# UNTIL I LEFT HOME

## Growing Up In
## Virginia's Shenandoah Valley
## In the 1920s And 1930s

### TWYMAN ELMORE BOWMAN

### MURPHY LORENZ PUBLISHING, LLC
Newark, Delaware

*Printed by*
**COMMERCIAL PRESS, INC.**
Stephens City, VA 22655

# UNTIL I LEFT HOME
## Growing Up In Virginia's Shenandoah Valley In The 1920s And 1930s

©Twyman Elmore Bowman 2004
ISBN 0-9753114-0-9

**MURPHY LORENZ PUBLISHING, LLC**
113 Barksdale Professional Center
Newark, Delaware 19711

## DEDICATED TO

My parents, Joyce Dellinger Bowman and Joseph Earl Bowman, and my brothers, Wilbur Alden Bowman and Dick Delford Bowman.

## ACKNOWLEDGMENTS

The contributions made by my wife, Lois Coleman Murphy Bowman, helped shape the contents of this book during its preparation from the original manuscript until the final product, for which I am grateful.

In addition, my stepdaughter, Janice Murphy Lorenz, who encouraged the transformation of a rough draft into a book, provided invaluable help with the typing, editing, and publishing necessary to bring the entire project to fruition.

Thanks also to my brother and sister in-law, Dick and Barbara Bowman, for their review and suggestions, and their contribution of many of the photographs.

Jim and Christion Murphy and Marilyn and Fred Anspach provided very much appreciated technical guidance.

Acknowledgments also are made to Douglas Foltz and Ray Salyer for their review and suggestions.

## Table of Contents

| Chapter | Contents | Page |
|---|---|---|
| 1 | Immediate Family................................... | 7 |
| 2 | Our Family – Three Generations............... | 14 |
| 3 | The Area ................................................... | 23 |
|   | Bridges ............................................ | 26 |
|   | Electric Power Service ...................... | 29 |
|   | Water Supply ................................... | 29 |
|   | Heating............................................. | 30 |
|   | Sundays ............................................ | 30 |
|   | Scenic Points ................................... | 31 |
|   | Architecture .................................... | 31 |
| 4 | Farming: The Major Industry ................... | 32 |
|   | Plowing ............................................ | 34 |
|   | Corn Planting ................................... | 37 |
|   | Corn Cultivation ............................... | 38 |
|   | Corn Harvesting ............................... | 30 |
|   | Grain Planting .................................. | 42 |
|   | Grain Harvesting .............................. | 43 |
|   | Grain Threshing ............................... | 44 |
|   | Hay Making ...................................... | 48 |
|   | Baling Hay ........................................ | 53 |
|   | Miscellaneous Farming Tasks .............. | 54 |
| 5 | Our Homes .......................................... | 59 |
|   | My Parents First Home ..................... | 59 |
|   | My Parents Second Home .................. | 63 |
|   | Grandmother Dellinger's Homes ......... | 73 |
|   | Grandpa & Grandma Bowman's Home . | 76 |

# Table of Contents

| Chapter | Contents | Page |
|---|---|---|
| 6 | Food............................................................... | 87 |
|  | Our Garden .......................................... | 87 |
|  | Cows and Milking ............................... | 96 |
|  | Meats and Pigs .................................... | 98 |
|  | Chickens and Eggs .............................. | 106 |
|  | Nuts, Fruits, Berries and Melons .......... | 110 |
|  | Sweets and Snacks ............................... | 113 |
| 7 | Work ............................................................. | 122 |
|  | The Garden .......................................... | 122 |
|  | Other Chores ........................................ |  |
| 8 | Play – One Boy, Two Boys, Three Boys ....... | 130 |
| 9 | Hunting and Trapping .................................. | 152 |
| 10 | Church .......................................................... | 158 |
| 11 | School ........................................................... | 162 |
|  | Hamburg Grade School ....................... | 162 |
|  | Triplett High School ........................... | 171 |
| 12 | Medical Care ................................................ | 176 |
| 13 | Travel and Transportation ............................ | 182 |
| 14 | Clothing ........................................................ | 190 |
| 15 | Socializing .................................................... | 195 |
| 16 | Fears, Dangers and Concerns ...................... | 201 |
| 17 | What to Do ................................................... | 205 |
| Epilogue | After I Left Home ........................................ | 212 |

## List of Figures

| Figure | Caption | Page |
|---|---|---|
| 1 | Joyce Dellinger Bowman and Joseph Earl Bowman ............................................... ….. | 12 |
| 2 | Immediate Family ....................................... | 13 |
| 3 | Joseph Earl Bowman ................................... | 20 |
| 4 | Grandmother and Grandfather Bowman and Baby Joseph Earl Bowman ......................... | 21 |
| 5 | Charles Dodson, Dorcas Dodson, Ellie Dodson, And Robert Dodson ...................... | 22 |
| 6 | Aerial View of Bowman Farm ...................... | 58 |
| 7 | Our Family Home ....................................... | 84 |
| 8 | Grandmother Dellinger's Second Home ……... | 85 |
| 9 | Grandfather and Grandmother Bowman's Home .................................................... | 86 |
| 10 | Grandmother Dellinger Splitting Wood ……... | 134 |
| 11 | Joseph Earl Bowman and His Hart Parr ……... | 135 |
| 12 | Dick Bowman and Twyman Elmore Bowman With Cow In Training ................................ | 150 |
| 13 | Twyman Elmore Bowman Riding Trained cow. | 151 |
| 14 | Otterbein Chapel United Methodist Church .. | 161 |
| 15 | Hamburg Three-Room Grade School ……… | 173 |
| 16 | Triplett High School, Mt. Jackson, Virginia ... | 174 |

## List of Figures

| Figure | Caption | Page |
|---|---|---|
| 17 | Twyman Elmore Bowman as High School Senior | 175 |
| 18 | Dick, TwymanElmore, and Alden Bowman | 223 |
| 19 | Twyman Elmore Bowman and Lois Coleman Murphy Bowman – 2003 | 224 |

Chapter One

## IMMEDIATE FAMILY

There were five members of my immediate family: my father, Joseph Earl Bowman; my mother, Joyce Augusta Dellinger Bowman; my older brother, Wilbur Alden Bowman; myself, Twyman Elmore Bowman; and my younger brother, Dick Delford Bowman.

All of our family was born in Ashby District, Shenandoah County, Virginia, within a three-mile radius. My father was born in Upper Hamburg in September, 1893. He attended Rochelle, a one-room grade school in Upper Hamburg, and later Hamburg Grade School in Lower Hamburg. He was the oldest living child in his family and was taken out of school after completing the fifth grade to work on the farm. This was more the rule than the exception, as farming was still very labor-intensive at that time because of the limited machinery available for farm use. Each of my father's five brothers and sisters completed grade school, several completed high school, and one graduated from college.

During the busy farm seasons my father worked on the farm planting, cultivating and harvesting crops. During the off-seasons he worked on the family-owned sawmills. The sawmills were moved from forest area to forest area because it was easier to transport sawed lumber to the customer than it was to transport logs to the sawmill.

While still a young man, my father operated machinery to do custom work for farmers in the immediate area consisting of a five-mile radius of his home. Custom work consisted of threshing grain, hulling hayseed, filling silos and baling hay. The threshing machine, clover huller, ensilage cutter and hay baler were towed from farm to farm by a steam engine, frequently referred to as a traction engine. The wood-fired steam engine also provided the belt power to drive the thresher, clover huller, ensilage cutter and the hay baler. Cleats on the rear wheel provided traction and the engine was steered with heavy chains attached to the ends of the front axles. The road speed of these engines was up to three miles per hour. The steam engine was also used to belt-power the sawmills. The Frick, Avery, and Aultman Taylor were three of these popular engines.

In 1928, my father purchased a used 28-50 Hart Parr gasoline powered tractor and an Avery threshing machine and went into business on his own instead of working for his family. My first memory (three years old) is of waiting all day for him to get home from Harrisonburg with the threshing rig. Toward evening, we saw and heard him come past Mr. Green Clanahan's farm, which was about four-tenths of a mile away, traveling at the Hart Parr's top speed of about four miles per hour. He continued to do custom work, adding an ensilage cutter and a hay baler to his machinery.

My father and mother married in December, 1920 at the Dellinger family home near Conicville, Virginia, about four miles from Hamburg. My mother attended the Teachers Normal, Madison College, to become qualified to teach in Virginia. That school is now known as James Madison University. I do not know the details of her schooling. She taught from 1911 to 1918 in a one-room school at Jerome, about six miles from her home. As was the custom, and the only practical thing to do, she roomed and boarded in a home at Jerome, which gave her pleasant family surroundings. The approximately thirty students at Jerome ranged in age from six to twenty-one.

Imagine the wide range of interest, ability and mischief that seven grades in one room could provide! She taught at Conicville in 1919 and 1920.

Controlling discipline was very difficult for many of the new teachers because the teachers were sometimes younger than the students. Many of the teachers went directly from grade school to the Normal for two years and then into teaching. Mother stated that she had only minor discipline problems because she got the upper hand early on. After taking a couple of the big boys by the collar and standing them in a corner the others fell in line so that some teaching could be accomplished. Some of the students thought she was somewhat psychic, because she could call the student down by name even if she was facing the blackboard! Her secret was that her glasses acted as rear-view mirrors so that the students did not have a chance!

My mother would frequently go to her mother's home on weekends, especially during pretty weather. She would walk the six miles home on Friday evening or Saturday morning and walk back on Sunday evening. If it snowed while she was home for the weekend, someone would take her back by buggy if the snow was not deep, or by horseback if the snow was deep. My father traveled by buggy while he was courting my mother.

Mother and Dad set up housekeeping in a house owned by Grandpa Bowman located next to the closed Rochelle Grade School, a half mile from my Grandfather's farm, where my father continued to work. Grandpa Bowman had bought the house and the three acres it sat on from his brother in-law, John, and rented it to my parents. My mother was relegated to the role of a housewife because in that day and time a married woman was not allowed to teach. My father was mostly involved in custom threshing, silo filling and baling hay and straw at this time.

Dr. Downey was our doctor, and with the help of a midwife, Alden was born December 8, 1921; myself ("Elmore") on July 18, 1925; and Dick on August 17, 1928. Alden and I were born at our first home, next to the closed Rochelle school, and Dick was born in the house that Mother and Dad built in 1925 and where they lived until their deaths. My first name "Twyman" is credited to the request of my mother's midwife. She must have disliked me even before I was born, and certainly afterwards, to have saddled me with a name like "Twyman," but my family always called me "Elmore." After leaving home I was known as "Bo," "Mo," and "Ty," with Ty being current.

Our family was not blessed with even one daughter, so Mother was thoughtful enough to allow us boys to do "girl work" such as washing dishes, dusting furniture, and scrubbing floors. We did not consider that this was really an "opportunity to excel," but, since it was our assignment, we did it. When we boys were working together and partially "lay-down" on the job, my mother would say "one boy is a whole boy, two boys is a half boy, and three boys is no boy at all." She was right.

The parent observing the need for discipline administered the discipline. Mother never threatened to "tell Dad when he came home;" she took care of the job herself because Dad left for work before we got up in the morning and frequently did not get home until seven or eight o'clock at night. Keen switches were always available behind the kitchen pitcher pump. There was no misunderstanding the reason or seriousness of the infraction, and I cannot remember any time that the discipline was unjustified. We boys were sent to the church yard next door to replenish the supply of switches when the old ones broke or became dry and brittle. There were hundreds of keen sprouts from the maple trees so the switch supply was inexhaustible; there was no reason to "spare the rod."

On one occasion when my brother was sent for switches, he notched the switches so that they would break the first time Mother struck him. He was sent back for another switch and then was given a double whipping, since Mother did not seem to appreciate his cleverness. That was known as the last of the "notched switches."

**Figure 1**
Joyce Dellinger Bowman & Joseph Earl Bowman

UNTIL I LEFT HOME 13

**Figure 2**
Immediate Family: Joseph Earl Bowman, Dick Delford Bowman, Twyman Elmore Bowman, Joyce Dellinger Bowman, and Wilbur Alden Bowman

## Chapter Two

## OUR FAMILY---THREE GENERATIONS

My father's parents were Martin Luther Bowman and Ida Rebecca Myers Bowman. My grandfather's two brothers were James Rufus Bowman and William Fisher Bowman, and his six sisters were Sarah Margaret Bowman, Mary Virginia Bowman, Elizabeth Frances Bowman, Rebecca Dyer Bowman, Josephine Dorcas Bowman, and Martha Ellen Bowman. I remembered little of my grandfather and his brothers and sisters, except seeing him leaning on our yard fence talking and laughing with my mother. I do remember coming home from school early to attend his funeral, which was in the spring of my second grade.

Grandmother Bowman's two brothers were Tom Myers and John Myers. Both owned farms adjacent to my grandmother's. Uncle Tom was married twice and had eighteen children spanning thirty-two years. Dick and I rode to Triplett High School with Uncle Tom, since he drove two of his youngest children to school. There were no school buses and five miles was a bit much to walk, even in those days. We never had any accidents, but there were some mighty close calls. Uncle John had two sons and four daughters, and their house was only about five hundred yards from my grandparents.

Grandma Bowman's sisters were Mollie Grim, who lived back of Woodstock; Sarah Carpenter, who lived in Hershey, Pennsylvania; and Pearl Foltz and Lucinda Heishman, both of whom lived near Conicville.

Grandpa and Grandma Bowman were farmers in Upper Hamburg, a half mile from where I was born and raised. They had eight children, their first being twins, a girl and boy; both died in infancy. Joseph Earl Bowman, my father, was the oldest of their surviving children. Grandpa Bowman was a good businessman and, as previously mentioned, he also owned another property consisting of a house and three acres, which he purchased from my Uncle John.

William Fred Bowman, their next oldest, never married and lived at their home place in Hamburg most of his life. He managed the farm for my grandmother after Grandpa Bowman's death, along with his own businesses. Uncle Fred was either part owner or full owner of businesses such as sawmills, grain and flour mills, other farms and a lumber business. He and Mr. Brown owned a lumberyard and were affectionately referred to as "Bark Edge Bowman" and "Knot Hole Brown." Although Uncle Fred never married, he never lacked the company of ladies and was frequently the subject of juicy gossip. He probably thought, "I wish I had as much fun as people give me credit for."

Roy Otis Bowman married Margaret Foltz. They built a home near Mt. Jackson, just up the road from the Civil War Veterans Cemetery. Uncle Roy was an Atlantic petroleum distributor for Mr. Shannon of Mt. Jackson, and later worked for the Gulf Oil Company distributorship. They had seven children: Eleanora, Louise, Chalmers, Beverly, Richard, Bill and Betty Jane. Alden, Dick and I had closer ties with Chalmers, since we all worked for Uncle Fred on the farm and Chalmers more frequently visited in our home. Both our work on the farm and the visits were fun times, but we always gave Uncle Fred a good day's work for a day's pay, and he treated us as adults.

Rebecca Mae Bowman who, like Uncle Fred, never married, also lived at the Bowman home place. She attended the National Business College at Roanoke, Virginia, and was the bookkeeper at the Edinburg Mill, owned by Uncle Fred and Dave Wilkins. This was a very old mill and one of the few mills in the Shenandoah Valley that was not burned by the Yankees during the Civil War. Aunt Mae quit working for the mill to take care of my grandmother Bowman when she was diagnosed with tuberculosis. Grandma lived on the first floor in a screened in porch, as the treatment for tuberculosis at that time was fresh air and rest.

Uncle Fred bought the Bowman home place when Grandma Bowman died, and he and Aunt Mae lived there until my brother, Dick, bought it in 1972. Then Uncle Fred and Aunt Mae bought a home just north of Mt. Jackson and lived there until their deaths.

Harry Guy Bowman married Kathryn Stout. He attended Roanoke College and the University of Virginia, getting a Masters degree in Finance. He worked for Shell Oil Company until he was conscripted into the Army just prior to World War II. He made a career of the Army, retired in 1971, and moved to Orlando, Florida. They had three children: Bruce, Roger and Nancy.

Bertie Ellen Bowman married Clarence Zirkle of New Market and lived and farmed on "Calabash Hill" near Quicksburg. Uncle Clarence farmed for many years and later was an insurance agent and also worked for the New Market newspaper. They had two children, Ernest and Luther.

My mother's father was Charles Peter Dellinger, and her mother was Mary Catherine Dodson Dellinger. Grandpa Dellinger worked in a bark camp in West Virginia, became ill with typhoid fever and died at the bark camp when my mother was less than five years old. Grandma never remarried, remained near Conicville, and raised their four children. I know very little about my grandfather because of his early death, 27 years before I was born. Grandpa and Grandma Dellinger lived on a small farm near Conicville with their four children, Joyce, Claude, Wilbur and Harold.

My Grandmother Dellinger's brothers were Robert Dodson ("Bob"), Jackson Dodson ("Jack"), and Charles Dodson ("Charlie"). Uncle Bob was a farmer and lived across the road and "crick" (creek) from my grandmother. The crick flowed down through Uncle Bob's farm, across the road, through my grandmother's yard and garden on into their neighbor's farm. Uncle Bob had four sons and no daughters. Uncle Bob's farm was one of the few farms in that area which was lighted by a carbide lighting system.

Uncle Jack lived near Conicville, previously called "Cabin Hill." Uncle Jack had three sons and two daughters. He was a farmer and also operated a kiln for producing charcoal, which in turn was used to melt iron in the pig iron furnaces of Shenandoah County.

Uncle Charlie lived in Manassas and owned a farm nearby. He worked for both the postal service and the railroad. Uncle Charlie had a great sense of humor, was never in a hurry and was loved by all who knew him. He had two sons and one daughter.

Grandmother Dellinger's three sisters were Dorcas, Ellie and Polly. Aunt Dorcas, a nurse, lived in Springfield, Ohio, and never married. She was very generous, and sent gifts to my grandmother, my mother and mother's brothers. She helped my grandmother financially during the years she was rearing the four children. After retiring from nursing, she made her home with Mother and Dad and died in our home.

Aunt Ellie Lutz moved to Navarre, Ohio, and had two sons and five daughters, all of whom were very close to my mother. Each visited her at least every two years. All of their family were loads of fun. They and their spouses had a great supply of jokes and were extremely witty. Aunt Polly never married and lived with my grandmother. Aunt Polly did the housework and Grandma did the outside work, such as garden, stock and chickens.

My mother, Joyce Augusta Dellinger Bowman, was the oldest of the Dellinger children and has already been mentioned. Her brother, Claude Dellinger, married Celia Shutters. Uncle Claude worked for the United States Postal Service, and lived in Washington, D.C., and Arlington, Virginia. He was extremely well respected in his profession, and was selected to make the initial trip from Washington, D.C., to Staunton when the mail bus system was inaugurated, replacing some of the mail rail system. They had two children, Claude and Madeline, who both lived in the Washington area. We were very close to the entire family even though they were one hundred miles away.

My mother's second brother, Wilbur ("Wib") Dellinger, married Stella Bowman, who was from a different line of Bowmans. Uncle Wib worked at the Mt. Jackson Post Office until illness forced him to quit. He was sick all the years that I knew him, but he always had a great sense of humor, even though he suffered terribly through his illness. They had one son, Charles, who lived in their home place near Conicville until his death.

Her third brother, Harold Dellinger, married Hildred Dellinger. There were two different lines of Dellingers. One of the traditions was that if two people married with the same surname, then the wife should bake bread for whooping cough victims. Aunt Hildred fulfilled those expectations. Uncle Harold worked at a variety of jobs both locally and in Washington, D.C., but always kept his residence at Conicville. They had one son, Walter, who lived in Washington, D.C.

**Figure 3**
Joseph Earl Bowman

**Figure 4**
Grandmother and Grandfather Bowman & baby Joseph Earl Bowman

**Figure 5**
Charles Dodson, Dorcas Dodson, Ellie Dodson Lutz & Robert Dodson

Chapter Three

## THE AREA

I was born and raised in the community of Hamburg, located between Mt. Jackson and Edinburg on what is now Shenandoah County Route 614 (South Middle Road). Mt. Jackson was originally Mt. Pleasant, but was later renamed Mount Jackson after Andrew Jackson. One of the stories of how Mt. Jackson got its name was that Robert E. Lee had a staff meeting and at the close of the meeting, Lee said "Mount, Jackson." This does not comport with Civil War history.

Other nearby communities were Rinkerton, Conicville, Headquarters, Hawkinstown and Bowman's Crossing. Shenandoah County is located in the Shenandoah Valley north of Harrisonburg and south of Winchester. The Appalachian Mountains are to the west and the Blue Ridge Mountains are to the east. Shenandoah County is about 13 miles wide and 40 miles long in a north-south direction. We referred to "going up" to Harrisonburg and "down" to Winchester, because the Shenandoah River flowed north from Harrisonburg toward Winchester. The county is bordered on the north by Frederick County, on the south by Rockingham County, on the east by Frederick and Page County and on the west by Hardy County of West Virginia.

Shenandoah County is divided into six districts, all about equal in size. The districts and the largest town in each area from north to south: Davis District—Strasburg; Stonewall District--Woodstock; Madison District—Edinburg; Ashby District--Mount Jackson; and Lee District--New Market, and Johnson District. The county seat of Shenandoah was located in the largest town, Woodstock, which was near the center of the county. The most well known historian who covered this area was Dr. John W. Wayland.

Hamburg, in the Ashby District, is an unincorporated community with no signs indicating where it starts or ends. The rolling land has a limestone rock base with considerable rock above the surface and who knows how much below grade. Shenandoah County was considered good farming country and farming has been and is the major occupation, causing the overall Shenandoah Valley to be referred to as "The Breadbasket of the Confederacy." Not only was the Valley fertile ground for food production for the Confederacy, many Civil War battles were fought in Shenandoah County, such as the Battle of Fishers Hill and the Battle of New Market. The Valley was laid waste by Sherman's Army in 1864. One of the few mills left unburned was the Edinburg Mill, which was later owned by my Uncle Fred and his first cousin, Dave Wilkins.

The Valley's various businesses, such as general stores, service stations, hardware stores, petroleum distributors, insurance, drug stores, farm machinery dealerships, and blacksmith shops supported the farming community.

When I was growing up, the major farm products in the area were wheat, corn, barley, hay, sheep, cattle, hogs and poultry. Many of the fields have so much limestone rock on or near the surface that the land could only be used for grazing and timber. It was impractical to grow crops requiring cultivation there because the rocks interfered with the use of plows, harrows, discs, mowers, binders, and cultivators.

The North Fork of the Shenandoah River flows north through Shenandoah County and joins the South Fork at Front Royal. The South Fork flows north through Elton and Luray, joins the North Fork at Front Royal and then flows to the Potomac River. The Shenandoah River was never used to handle cargo or transport passengers.

The Shenandoah River is fed by creeks, which flow into it from the direction of the Allegheny and Blue Ridge Mountains. Two of these streams are Mill Creek and Stoney Creek, which joined the North Fork of the Shenandoah at Mt. Jackson and Edinburg, respectively. These creeks supplied water power to the several mills located beside them.

The creeks were dammed upstream of the mill, the distance depending on the "fall" of the creek. The concrete dams were normally no more than ten feet high with their length dependent on the width of the creek. A mill race was constructed to carry the water from the dam to the mill water wheel. The mill races were all earth except at the dam and at the mill end. The water wheels to power the mills were of the type that depends on the weight of the water to develop the torque to drive the milling machinery. The elevation of the dam relative to the mill was small, which was the reason that this type of water wheel was used.

Steam engines or gasoline powered engines or tractors could be used to power the mill if the water system or water wheel drive was out-of-service. The dam and/or mill race could be out-of-service due to dam damage, race damage, or severe freezing. The water wheel system could be damaged by water wheel bearing failure, water wheel bucket damage, shafting problems and water control gates.

The major raw materials supplied to the mill were wheat, corn, barley, rye and oats, and the output products were flour, bran, mash for poultry, cracked grain, scratch feed, corn meal, hog feed and middlins (a mixture of flour and bran). The farmer could pick up the mill products at the mill or the mill would deliver them. The farmers would take grain, such as wheat, to the mill and would have it ground and mixed for their farm use.

General stores served the farming communities and those serving the Hamburg community were Edgar Rosenberger's store at Bowman's Crossing (closed in early 1940s), Eckard's Store, located near Hamburg Grade School (closed in early 1930s); Painters Store on Route 614 about one half-mile from my home; and Foltz's Store in Lower Hamburg were in operation during my youth. Mt. Jackson and Edinburg, the two nearest towns, had stores that offered more variety and services than the general stores, such as hardware, clothing, banking, coal and fertilizer.

**Bridges**

We traveled on state, county and private roads and forded the streams or crossed on bridges. The four general types of bridges were the swinging bridge, the covered bridge, the open bridge, and the submarine bridge. Swinging bridges were used only for people to walk across, as they were too small and too weak for vehicular travel. These bridges consisted of two strong cables stretched across the stream and anchored on each side. A level-walking platform of boards was suspended below the large cables by wires. Wires were also run along both sides of the platform up to about three feet above it to hold on to and to prevent falling off the walkway. If you walked carefully across the bridge, there was a minimum of motion of the walking surface, but unless accompanied by adults, boys did not walk carefully.

We would run, jump, sway and play on the bridge so that it would go up and down and swing from side to side. The motion of the bridge caused wear as it increased the stresses on the structural members and could result in bridge failure. The swinging bridge at Narrow Passage was one of the longest and highest in the area and a popular place for couples to go when dating.

Covered bridges in the area were constructed almost entirely of wood with the roof and sides closed in to minimize the weather damage. The roof, sides and travel surface provided the structural strength to support the weight between the abutments and center structure supports, if any. Many of the covered bridges were wide enough for traffic in one direction only; therefore, whoever got to the bridge first, crossed and the other traveler waited.

There is still one operational covered bridge in Shenandoah County, located just off of and west of US Route 11 on Route 720 south of Mt. Jackson at Meems Bottom. Relatively flat land beside the river was prime farmland, producing better crops than the rolling and hilly land and was referred to as "river bottom." This was the only land that could be irrigated because there was no other large supply of water. Meems Bottom was the largest river bottom farm in Shenandoah County.

Open bridges were constructed of either logs or steel. Those across small streams of thirty feet or less were supported by logs spanning the entire width of the creek bed. Thick boards were placed across these logs to form the driving surface of the bridge. Heart timber was used for these bridges to minimize deterioration due to the weather, as well as the abrasive use. The open bridges across larger streams were usually steel, with the overhead structure, the side structure and the road surface structure forming a large strength unit. These were set on abutments made of stone or concrete. The road surface was either wood or tar and gravel, depending on availability of material. These steel bridges were used across the Shenandoah River and other large streams such as Mill Creek and Stoney Creek.

Covered and open bridges were located above the expected flood level of the streams so that floodwater would not damage them. The bridge abutments had to be deep and strong enough so that they would not be damaged during the flooding. Heavy rains and rapid snow melting on the farms and in the mountains, adding to the streams, caused the floods. Floating debris such as trees and buildings, which had been washed off their foundations and carried downstream, frequently damaged the bridges. The bridges were often impassable during flood conditions, since the approach roads to the bridges were lower than the bridges.

The fourth type of bridge was known as the submarine bridge, aptly named, as it would be flooded over during high water conditions. Submarine bridges were all concrete construction and built close to the normal water level. The submarine bridge may be damaged by low floating debris or partially plugged up by trees and other heavy objects. This debris had to be cleared out as the floodwater receded so that the submarine would be passable. Even moderately high water flooded over the bridge, making it impassable.

Culverts were used on small streams and were a form of submarine bridge. They consisted of one or more pipes installed below the road level and perpendicular to the traffic flow to carry the water. The pipes were covered with soil and rocks over which the people and vehicles moved. These also flooded over during high water conditions.

**Caves**

There were many caves throughout this limestone country, varying in size from very small to large commercial ones such as Endless Caverns at New Market and Shenandoah Caverns at Mt. Jackson. Many of the local residents, especially young people, explored these off-the-beaten-path caves as recreation. There were many more cave explorations made sitting around the country store, at school, at church and wherever people gathered than there were at the cave sites. We frequently planned to explore the caves near Pleasant View Church but never got beyond the talking stage. I guess we were smarter than we realized, as cave exploration can be extremely dangerous even for experienced spelunkers.

**Electric Power Service**

The first electric power service in the county was Virginia Public Service. The lines ran along the major roads and if the home was more than about 100 feet from the road the resident had to pay for the line to the house. The stem line to my Grandmother Bowman's home was one half mile which was at her expense. The power line came by our home but we did not have electricity installed until 1935. The REA (Rural Electrification Administration) came in many years later and ran electric lines to people off the main road, making electricity more affordable. Electric refrigerators made the farmers' ice houses obsolete.

## Water Supply

Cisterns, creeks, springs, wells and ponds provided farm water. Cisterns, springs and wells provided household water and ponds could be used only for stock and poultry because of water impurity. Cisterns were filled by rain water run off of the buildings in lieu of wells as well drilling was extremely expensive and a gamble. The well drilling rigs were somewhat primitive and extremely slow. If you hit rock, which you frequently did, you could only drill a few feet per day, as the drilling rig had to chisel through the rock. Springs were a convenient source of water if they happened to be at the right place and if they continued flowing during dry weather. Wet-weather springs flowed only during seasonally wet weather.

## Heating

Almost all homes were heated with wood or coal. The wood was from nearby forests and the coal came in from southwest Virginia, West Virginia and Pennsylvania. The wood cook stoves made the kitchens extremely hot during the summer cooking and canning season. Some homes used coal oil (kerosene) stoves for summer cooking and canning to decrease the heat in the kitchen.

## Sundays

Only necessary work was done on Sundays. The area was mostly Protestant with many denominations such as Lutheran, Methodist, Reform, United Brethren, and Baptist. Work on Sunday consisted of cooking for the family, feeding the cows, horses, chickens, etc. Of course, the cows had to be milked twice a day, the eggs gathered, and the stock and poultry watered and fed.

**Scenic Points**

We always appreciated the many scenic points that provided beautiful views of the Shenandoah Valley and surrounding mountains, and would take company to enjoy the view from points such as the fire towers overlooking the seven bends in the Shenandoah River, Rudes Hill overlooking Meems Bottom, and Signal Mountain near Strasburg. The Civil War Veterans Cemetery at Mount Jackson always had services on special occasions such as the Fourth of July and Memorial Day that we also enjoyed attending.

**Architecture**

Homes in the Hamburg community were not pretentious, and our family homes were no exception. However, my great uncle Tom's home was the oldest in the area and of frame construction. The fact that local forests served as the source of building materials made frame houses more economical than brick or stone. It should also be noted that it is quite an honor that my great, great, great, great, great Grandfather Bowman's home, built about 1732, is being moved to the Frontier Cultural Center near Staunton as an example of German architectural influences in the Shenandoah Valley.

Chapter Four

# FARMING: THE MAJOR INDUSTRY

The major industry of the area was farming, with the average small farm consisting of about one hundred acres. There were a few farms larger than 1,000 acres, such as Meems Bottom. The following describes the small farm of my grandparents, which was typical of most small farms. The farm acreage division was about fifteen acres for corn, fifteen acres for wheat, thirty acres for hay, thirty acres for grazing and woods, and the remaining land for the house, barn, garden, lanes, barnyard, hog yard and outbuilding. It was on rolling land with too much limestone rock both underground and above ground for all of it to be effectively farmed. This rocky land was used for grazing or forest.

**Farm Management**

Farms were operated in three distinct ways relative to labor; however, the actual farming techniques were the same for all three management methods. One method was operation by the owner and his family, with hired help, or "help-for-help-back" for big jobs such as threshing, hay baling and silo filling. Another method was tenant farmers, and the third method was through the use of yearly help.

On farms owned and operated by the family, father and sons did the outside work, while the mother and daughters did the inside work and the gardening. The women frequently helped out in the field doing work that did not require the strength of a man, such as raking hay, loading hay, loading wheat and driving the horse to pull the hayfork. Neighbors and hired day help were used for the jobs requiring more help than the family members could do. Much of the neighbor help was "help for help back," and at some convenient time, the differences in help effort were negotiated and a cash equalizing settlement made. The day help received about a dollar a day if the family furnished dinner (noon meal) and a dollar and a quarter if the worker furnished his own dinner.

In a tenant farming arrangement, the tenant farmer furnished all of the labor and machinery and half of the seed and fertilizer, whereas the farm owner provided the land and buildings, kept the buildings in repair, paid the taxes and half of the seed and fertilizer. The owner and the tenant shared the profits from the crops on a fifty-fifty basis. The tenant had the use of the garden and was permitted to raise chickens, hogs for butchering, and could keep one or two cows for milk. The tenant, with the agreement of the owner, frequently raised additional stock such as cattle and hogs. The expenses and profit were shared between the owner and the tenant, as agreed to in their yearly contract, which could be verbal or written. The tenant farmer frequently worked the farm for many years, which indicated that the arrangement was mutually beneficial.

On farms managed by a tenant overseer, the owner hired a yearly tenant to work and oversee the work of other farm employees. My Grandmother Bowman's farm was operated in this manner. The tenant overseer furnished only his time and labor and the owner furnished the farm, machinery, seed and fertilizer. The owner controlled the work schedule and made the major decisions about plant selection. The tenant overseer received about twenty-five or thirty dollars a month and was given a house to live in, a garden, one milk cow, two hogs for butchering, and other incentives such as flour and feed for the cow and hogs. The tenant overseer would usually stay with the same farm family for many years, as did Lester Donovan and his family, who stayed with my Grandmother Bowman about eight years.

Regardless of the type of farm management, farming entailed a six-day week, with necessary work also being done on Sundays. Sunday work was milking, feeding the stock, and watering the stock that did not have access to water at all times. The tenant responsible for a monthly tenant-operated farm was completely responsible for the entire farm operation. If the tenant wanted to be away on a Sunday, he would have to make arrangements with the farm owner or a neighbor so that the essential work would be done. Uncle Fred or my father frequently filled in on Sunday for my grandmother's tenant.

### Plowing

The work performed on the farms was the same for all three farm management arrangements. Crop rotation was used to keep from "wearing out" the land by continuing to plant the same crop in the same field year after year.

A typical crop rotation was corn the first year, wheat or barley the second year, and hay the following two years. The land was plowed every four years prior to corn planting by using single-bottom turning plows pulled by two, three or four horses. The number of horses used was dependent upon the soil condition, moisture, plow size, size of the horses and the availability of horses. The plow turned a furrow eight to ten inches wide and about six to eight inches deep. A rule of thumb was to try to turn up a half inch of subsoil each time the land was plowed.

One man operated the plow and controlled the horses using a lead line. A lead line connects to both ends of the bit in one horse's mouth and is connected together and brought back to the operator as one line. The line going to the left end of the bit is slightly shorter than the one going to the right side. Lead poles connect the other horses to control their direction. To direct the horses to go left (haw) the operator would pull on the line. To direct the horses to go right (gee), the operator would jerk the line. The horses usually only needed guidance at turns, as the lead (left) horse walked in the furrows.

Plow parts were made of either cast iron or steel, with the steel parts being about three times as expensive as the cast parts. Steel parts could have the cutting point replaced by the blacksmith, and the steel point would not break when the plow hit a rock. The cast iron plow points had to be thrown away when they became dull, worn or broken.

The plow operator had to be very alert to prevent damaging the plow when it hit a rock or tree root on or near the surface. A good plow horse would automatically stop when it felt or heard the plow strike a rock. A plow could be sprung or broken from hitting just one rock because the plow beam was either steel or wood. The moisture condition of the soil was extremely important. If the soil was too dry, the plow would be very difficult to pull; therefore less land could be plowed in a day because the horses had to be rested more. In addition, dry ground was very abrasive to the plow point and caused more wear on the moldboard, so that the plow point required frequent replacement. This increased the cost of plowing.

The plowed land was then worked to crush the clods, level the ground and soften it for planting. The equipment used to prepare the soil for planting was the disc harrow, drag harrow, drags, cultipackers and spring tooth harrow. The disc harrow had four cutting sections with each containing five to seven discs. The discs in each section were bolted together with six-inch spacers between the discs. The front two sections were adjusted to push the soil away from the center of the disc, and the two rear sections were adjusted to pull the soil toward the center of the disc. This cutting helped keep the soil level as well as cut the soil in two directions.

The drags were made of timbers, which were perpendicular to the direction of travel and spaced a few inches apart. The timbers cut the tops off of the protruding clods, leaving the surface smooth. The drag harrow was a tool made of timbers about five inches square and secured together with considerable space between them. The timbers had harrow teeth through them protruding about five inches out of the bottom. As the drag harrow was pulled across the field, it acted as a drag (described above) and also cultivated the soil about five inches deep. The teeth were arranged and the drag harrow pulling angle adjusted so that the teeth did not track, one behind the other, so that all of the soil was loosened.

The cultipackers broke up the clods by rolling "V" shaped rollers over the clods to break them up. This rolling action tended to pack the soil and had to be followed by a disc harrow, drag harrow or spring tooth harrow. The spring tooth harrow was a sled-like tool with small shovels. The shovels were each mounted to a spring bent roughly in a semi-circle. The other end of the spring was connected to an operating mechanism, which controlled the depth of the teeth, which were adjusted to penetrate the soil. The spring-tooth harrow only loosened the soil; therefore it was frequently the last implement used prior to planting the corn.

**Corn Planting**

The corn was planted using a two-row corn planter, which was pulled by two horses and operated by one man. Three of the corn planter manufacturers were McCormick, Deere and Oliver. The operator rode the corn planter and guided the horses using check lines. Check lines consist of leather lines connected to both ends of both horses' bits. The two right ends are then connected to a line back to the operator. The two left ends are connected similarly. A steady pull on the right line turns the horse's right, and a steady pull on the left line turns the horses left.

The corn planter has two cylindrical containers for corn, one located over each row. There are two larger containers for fertilizer, located behind the corn containers. The contents of both the containers was dropped in a furrow at the same time and covered. The furrow was opened by one or two discs or by a boot, which opened up the furrow. The soil fell back to close the furrow, thus covering the kernels and fertilizer. The corn planters could be set to plant the corn in rows or in hills.

Corn intended for use as silage (chopped corn stored in a tight container to be used as cattle feed) was sowed in rows with a kernel of corn planted about every foot. The rows were usually three feet apart but could be adjusted closer if desired. Rich soil could support more stalks for a given area than could poorer ground.

Corn intended for growth to maturity was planted in rows three feet apart in hills. Two or three kernels of seed corn were planted in each hill, and if all three came up, one stalk was removed (thinning), so that each hill contained two stalks. This was determined to be the best method from a production standpoint based on years of experience on this farm and on most other farms. The hills were arranged so that the corn could be cross-cultivated (cultivated in the direction of planting and at right angle to this) thereby eliminating the necessity to hoe out the weeds. This was called "planting the corn in check." Checking was accomplished by stretching a wire chain the length of the field, which tripped the planters at the proper time to drop the kernels. The chain had to be moved each time the end of the row was reached. Adjusting and setting the chain required skill and experience to achieve hills of corn which could be cultivated in both directions.

**Corn Cultivation**

We cultivated our corn five to six times during the growing season. The cultivation was in the same direction each time for the corn sowed in rows, but for corn planted in check, we changed the direction of cultivation each time it was cultivated. This eliminated weeds, which otherwise could have grown between the hills.

The corn was cultivated when it was less than about two feet tall by either a two-horse one-row riding-cultivator or by one horse pulling a double- or triple-shovel plow cultivating one side of one row at each pass. The operator who sat behind the front plow shovel controlled the riding cultivator. The plow shovels could be directed by the direction of the horses for general positioning. The operator could exert pressure on the plow assembly with his legs to reposition the plows a few inches to perform the fine positioning. This was especially necessary when cultivating at right angles to planting, for no checking is perfect.

The double and triple-shovel cultivators had to be used after the corn stalks were greater than about two feet tall because the two-horse cultivator would break the corn stalks over. The last cultivation of the season was after the corn was quite tall, and it was not unusual for the corn to be as high as the horse and man. The horses had to be rested frequently during any farm work, especially during this cultivation, which was more severe because there was essentially no air movement in the tall corn. The operator walked behind the plow with one hand on each cultivator handle and controlled the horse using a lead line. Two-row cultivators were used when tractors became available in the late 1930s and early 1940s. Companies such as Oliver, Deere, Case and Farmall manufactured the farm implements.

The corn was thinned when small by pulling all but two stalks out of each hill and tamping dirt against the hill to cover any exposed corn roots. If the roots were not properly covered or the farmer did not cultivate the corn following thinning, some of the corn might die. Each time the corn was cultivated the soil was pushed up against the corn hill to prevent root exposure and hopefully smother out small weeds.

## Corn Harvesting

The corn was harvested in September while it was still green if it was to be used for ensilage. The ears were not fully matured when it was harvested. However, some farmers pulled the ears before cutting the stalks for ensilage. These ears were usually fed to the hogs. The corn stalks were cut using a hand corn chopper, and then placed on piles. Each man had his own personal hand chopper and each thought his chopper was better than anyone else's. Some hand choppers were similar to machete; another was a form of knife located on the end of a wood handle at an angle to suit the person, and variations of these. The piles of corn were picked up and loaded on low ensilage wagons to be hauled to the ensilage cutter. The low wagons were easier to load and unload than the standard hay wagon.

The ensilage cutter had a short conveyor to carry the corn stalks (bottom first) into the ensilage rollers and cutters. The ensilage cutter was driven at high revolutions per minute to chop up the corn into pieces about one inch long. A large blower fan blew the chopped corn up the pipe and down into the silo. A popular ensilage cutter was the Papec. Water was frequently run into the ensilage as it was being chopped, which made the job of tamping the ensilage in the silo miserable.

Two men usually worked in the silo, which was a tough job at best. If down pipes were not used in the silo, the job was even more unpleasant as the chopped corn just rained down on the men. We always used down pipes. The silos varied in diameter from eight to twenty feet and in height from thirty to sixty feet. The one on my grandmother's farm was about ten feet in diameter and forty feet tall, and required one day to fill.

The corn that was grown to maturity was cut and shocked in the field. The saddle (center support) of the shock consisted of tying the tops of four hills of corn together near the top of their stalks. The other hills of corn were cut off near the ground and stacked against the saddle with the tassel ends up. Different farmers had different ways of cutting and shocking corn. A popular way was to put a sixteen-hill square on one shock, which means that there were about five hundred stalks per shock. Each stalk usually had one or two ears.

The corn stalks were handled in basically two ways. One way was to cut the stalks and put them in piles which were later picked up and put against the saddle. The other method was called "hugging" which consisted of cradling several hills of corn (one at a time) in one arm and chopping the corn stalks off with the other hand. The armful of corn is then carried and placed on the shock. This continued until the shock was complete. The corn shock would then be tied about two-thirds of the way up so that the ears and stalks would not be damaged by rain, snow and wind.

Some farmers had corn harvesters, which cut the corn stalks and left them on the ground in untied bundles. The bundles were then picked up and placed on shocks. The corn ears were usually shucked off the corn shock in the field and the ears of corn put in the corn crib for further processing, such as grinding in a hammer mill, and then fed to the cattle, horses and hogs. The corn stalks were fed to the cattle as roughage, and that not eaten was used for bedding in the barnyard.

## Grain Planting

After the corn was cut and shocked the soil was tilled to prepare the field for planting grain, such as wheat or barley. A disc harrow, which was frequently pulled by three or four horses, usually tilled the land. All of the land was cultivated except the area under the corn shocks, which was about eight feet in diameter. The harrowing operation had to be carefully done to balance between loosening the soil enough to accept the seed, and not tearing the corn stalk stubble loose from the soil. Tearing the stubble loose would delay the rotting process of the corn roots, but more importantly, the stubble would catch on the grain drill and cause uneven sowing of the seed. The grain was sown using a two-horse drill and one operator, who would walk behind the drill to ensure that the grain and fertilizer were properly sown.

The drill had two large-diameter wheels, which provided the driving power for the drill mechanism. The drill mechanism fed the grain and fertilizer into the soil. It was about eight feet wide and sowed about twenty rows of grain and fertilizer at a time. The two types of drills were the "disk" and the "boot." The basic difference was how the small furrow was made to accept the grain and fertilizer. The "disk" type had rotating disks, at a small angle to the direction of travel, which opened a furrow, dropped the seed and fertilizer in the furrow, which fell closed. The "boot" type plowed open a small furrow, dropped the seed and fertilizer and the furrow fell closed to cover both. The disk drill would tend to roll over debris such as corn stubble, whereas the boot drill would tend to rake up debris.

Grain was planted either in the fall or spring, the fall crop generally producing a greater yield. A very good yield was about thirty bushels per acre; however, the average yield was between twenty and thirty-five bushels. The yields were directly related to the weather--one year following a hailstorm, my grandmother's field yielded only four bushels per acre. Many people did not even harvest the wheat that year.

**Grain Harvesting**

Grain was harvested in June and early July, with barley becoming ripe about two weeks ahead of the wheat. It was very important that the grain be harvested at its proper time relative to ripeness. If the grain was harvested too soon, the grains were not mature and were much less valuable for both the market and for horses, cows, hogs and poultry feed. If the grain was too ripe, the kernels might fall out during the cutting, shocking and hauling, thereby losing a portion of the crop. Large sheets were sometimes placed on a wagon crane to catch the grain that was lost during loading and hauling. The wagon crane was an open bed placed on the wagon running gear to hold hay and grain.

Over-ripe stalks may bend over and lodge, making it impractical to gather all of the stalks and thus losing a portion of the yield. When hay, such as timothy, was harvested for seed, the same difficulties existed as did for the grain. The timothy got too ripe one year, and to avoid losing much of the seed, we harvested after dark when the dew was on the timothy. This fortunately occurred during full moon, which was the only light that we had, except those on the tractor.

Grain was harvested using a binder pulled by three or four horses and, in later years, by tractor, all before the combine era. The two operations associated with harvesting were operating the binder and shocking the grain. The binder operation was performed by either one or two men and the shocking by two to four men. The two-man binder operation consisted of one man driving the three-horse team, and the other man manipulating the binder.

All of the functions of the binder operator were mechanically done through shafting, linkages and levers. These functions included adjusting the height of the cutter bar; the height and position of the reel so that the grain would fall on the canvass conveyor belt properly, the size of the sheaves, dropping the sheave in a row for easy shocking and other binder operations. Frequently, one man would both operate the binder and drive the team. My great Uncle Tom was still the binder operator on his farm at the age of 76, which was quite unusual because of his advanced age.

The sheaves were put on shocks to allow curing and drying of the grain kernels and the stalks. The shocks were constructed so that rain would not damage the grain while curing and waiting for the thresher. The shock consisted of three sheaves standing in a row, with the grain heads up, two sheaves on each side of the first row and two sheaves on the top called caps. The cap sheaves were broken by bending the stalks and shaping them so that water would flow off the shock rather than into it.

### Grain Threshing

Separating the grain from the stalk and the chaff was called threshing. The grain was either "field threshed" or put in the barn for "barn threshing." Field threshing was done in July and August and barn threshing was done in

September and October. Each method had advantages and disadvantages, so each farmer picked the method which suited him. Field threshing required no building to store the grain in before threshing, but needed more manpower on thresh day than did barn threshing. The overall labor was greater for barn threshing because in barn threshing the grain had to be handled twice, first when it was put in the barn, and later when it was taken out on thresh day. The extra labor time was favorable to large farm families, as they had to rely less on non-family help.

The thresher was a rectangular-shaped machine about ten feet high, eight feet wide and twenty-five feet long, powered by a tractor or steam engine via a flat belt about seven inches wide and sixty feet long. The sheaves were thrown on the feeder conveyor belt, which carried the sheaves into the knives. The knives were reciprocating rotating blades on four assemblies with each assembly having six knives. The knives cut the binder twine off the sheaves and mangled the grain stalks so that they were carried into the spikes to dislodge the grain from the grain heads.

The stalks (straw) and chaff were separated from the grain by shakers and blowers down the length of the thresher. A large diameter blower at the rear of the thresher blew the straw and chaff out of the machine. The grain was carried to the top of the thresher by an auger in a pipe, weighed and dumped down the pipe into bags for carrying to the granary for storage.

Field threshing was usually done by placing the thresher in the barn and hauling the sheaves of grain from the field to the barn. Another method was to locate the thresher outside the barn. The thresher location depended on what was the best way to handle the two products from the thresher; the grain and the straw. The straw was blown in a pile to form a straw rick and the grain was put in a granary. It was desirable to locate the straw rick near the stock pens since it was used for bedding throughout the year. This was frequently the deciding factor. Many of the bank barns located the thresher in the barn close to both the granary and the barnyard and where the straw rick was most desirable.

A bank barn had a lower level for the animals and a higher overhead upper level for hay and grain storage. The lower level had a dirt or gravel floor and the upper level had a wooden floor. The barn was frequently located backed up to a hill with large rolling doors on both the back and front side. The loaded wagons were driven in the barn's back doors, which were nearer the level of the barn floor; therefore, the incline was smaller.

If the barn was located on near level ground, a dirt and rock barn bridge was built with a small incline. This small incline made it easier for the teams to pull the wagons into the barn for unloading. The large doors on the front of the barn, facing the barnyard, were used when threshing and sometimes when feeding the cattle hay. The rear end of the thresher usually stuck out of the barn to allow better movement of the thresher blower. The silo was usually beside the barn so that less effort was required to feed ensilage to the cattle.

The sheaves of grain were loaded on three or four horse-drawn wagons by two men who pitched the sheaves onto the wagon, and by two people who put the sheaves in place. The wagons were equipped with cranes for hauling which are described under Hay Making. If four teams were used, the horses remained hitched to the same wagon and just stood there while the wagon was unloaded into the threshing machine. Three-team operation required that as soon as the wagon was pulled alongside the thresher, the horses were unhitched from this wagon and hitched to the wagon that had just been unloaded. Sometimes it was necessary to use five wagons and another team if the field was more distant from the thresher.

Field threshing could require as many as twenty-one men for one day. There were six or nine men in the field loading the wagons, three or four men driving the teams, two men feeding the thresher, two men bagging and storing the threshed grain, two men on the straw rick and two men operating the threshing rig. The earlier threshing machines were powered by steam engines, such as the Aultman-Taylor, Frick and Avery. Gasoline-fueled tractors replaced practically all of the steam engines by 1930. My father used a Hart Parr 28/50 tractor and Avery thresher after 1928.

The men feeding the thresher pitched the sheaves, head end first, onto the feeder conveyor, which carried the sheaves into the thresher knives. These knives were driven by a crank shaft, which rotated the knives in a reciprocating motion to cut the binder twine and loosen up the grain stalks of the sheave. The sheaves then went through the thresher, which knocked the grains out of the heads and separated them from the stalks and chaff. The grain was automatically weighed and dumped into bags. The straw and chaff were blown out of the blower pipe by a fan located within the rear end of the thresher. The blower operator traveled with the thresher and directed the straw to suit the men making the straw rick.

Once in a while, a ricker would make nasty comments to the blower operator. This was not too smart, as the blower operator could chase the ricker off of the rick by directing the straw directly at him. That usually solved the problem. The second thresher operator, usually the owner, continuously monitored the tractor and thresher operation to get the most quantity and cleanest grain from the heads.

Barn threshing required about ten men to perform all tasks. There were four or five men required to move the sheaves to the thresher, two men to bag and move the grain, two more on the rick and the two thresher operators. Feeding the thresher was a crucial operation, as feeding too many sheaves too fast, or feeding them cross-wise on the conveyor could choke the thresher. If that occurred, the thresher non-rotating sets of spikes had to be disassembled to remove the excess stalks and then reassembled. If the stalks were not dry, the thresher was more likely to choke, and then time was wasted.

**Hay Making**

Hay crops followed the grain crops in the crop rotation sequence. Hay seed was sown either before or after the harvesting of the grain, and the soil was not cultivated prior to sowing the seed. "Broadcasting" using a hand-cranked spreader, such as the Cyclone spreader, was frequently used to sow hay seed. The operation of the spreader required skill to get an even distribution of the seed and thus an even stand of hay. It was not unusual to see a field of hay which revealed exactly where the seed sower walked as he broadcast the seed. The hay was allowed to grow until the quantity and quality were correct and then it was mowed with a sickle-bar mower.

Two horses pulled the mower with the mower operator riding the mower and driving the horses with check lines.

A mower was much simpler to operate than a binder, as there was only the height and tilt of the sickle bar that had to be adjusted. The team was operated so that there was no uncut hay, and at the same time, a full cutter bar cut was made to minimize the number of passes that had to be made. The hay was left lying on the ground until it was dry enough to put in the hay mow, or on a hay rick.

Some farmers used hay tedders, pulled by one or two horses, which had two- or three-prong forks operated from a crank shaft to kick the hay stalks apart to hasten and more evenly dry the hay. This was needed more if the hay was very dense, for the hay on top would be too dry before the hay on the bottom got dry enough. If a farmer had no tedder, the men would walk through the hay field and turn the hay over using pitchforks. When the hay was of the right dryness, it was then ready to be put in the barn or on the hay rick. The hay was later fed to the cows, horses and sheep or baled and sold as a direct money crop.

The determination of the correct dryness and toughness of the hay was extremely important. If it was allowed to become too dry, many of the nutrients were lost and the hay would have a brown color rather than the slightly green color desired. Brown hay had a lower sale value because the food value of the hay was less than hay that was properly cured. If the hay was put in the hay mow or on a hay rick when it was too green, excessive heat might be produced. The heat could become so great that it would spontaneously combust the hay rick, and possibly burn the barn down.

There were several levels of heating depending on the condition and the amount of hay involved. The lowest level of heat was that which caused no damage to the hay itself or anything else. The second level was when the heat was hot enough that it damaged the quality of the hay, thereby decreasing its usefulness, but did not ignite in flames. Occasionally, there were cases in which the heat became intense enough that the hay smoldered but did not break out into flames. It may leave a smoldered-out hole in the hay, which would not be discovered until the hay was removed for feeding. That was described as a "close call," and you can be sure that next year the hay would be drier when it was put in the hay mow or rick.

The third level of heat occurred when the heat of the hay grew so great that flames broke out and caught the barn on fire. An accidental fire was one of the most feared tragedies on the farm.

Hay was gathered from the field basically by two methods: raking and manually pitching the hay on the wagon, or by using a mechanical hay loader. Two horses pulled the hay wagon using the manually pitching method, but the wagon with the hay loader behind it required three horses to satisfactorily pull it. The pick-up hay-baler was also coming into use, but it will not be described. The raking and manually pitching the hay method is described.

A one-horse buggy rake or a two-horse side-delivery rake was used to rake the hay into windrows (a continuous roll of hay). A boy about ten years or older could handle this job, freeing someone stronger for heavier tasks. The men frequently made the windrows into piles, which were easier to pitch onto the wagon. The mechanical hay loaders picked the hay off the windrow or directly from the ground if the hay was heavy.

The hay was loaded onto the wagons and hauled to the barn or hay rick. The wagons were pulled by two horses, had four wooden-spoked wheels with steel rims and were outfitted with a crane instead of a bed. The crane was a wooden framework set on the running gear of the wagon to support the hay. A "standard" (pole) was mounted at each of the four corners to keep the hay from sliding off the wagon. The crane was about eight feet wide and twenty-four feet long. If the rims or spokes became loose, the wheels were removed and put in the horse trough overnight to swell up the wood, a temporary repair.

Hay was pitched onto the wagon and one man or boy placed or tamped the hay in place. The hay overhung the sides of the wagon by about one foot, making the load about ten feet wide. The horses required little driving during this type of hay loading, as they responded to verbal commands from the man on the wagon or one of the men on the ground. The height of the hay on the wagon was six to eight feet above the crane, with the crane being greater than three feet off the ground.

If the men pitching the hay were skillful, strong and conscientious, the loader had little to do except tamp the hay. Several wagons may be loaded before any of them were taken to be unloaded. The number of men, wagons and horses, and the likelihood of rain determined this. If hay is rained on after it is mowed and before it is taken into the barn, more drying time is necessary, which lowers the hay quality. Repeated rains may completely ruin the hay, making it only good for bedding.

The mechanical hay loader was pulled behind the wagons and the long oscillating rakes ratcheted the hay up the loader and discharged it onto the wagons, which were loaded from the back to the front. Usually two men did the loading and one man drove the team. Skilled loaders would let the hay loader do much of the work, reducing the degree of manual labor required. The skill of the loader also made a great deal of difference in how tangled the hay became and thus how difficult it was to unload and place in the hay mow or rick and later remove for feeding.

The loaded hay wagons were pulled onto the barn floor for unloading into the hay mow. The barns were usually "bank barns" with an earth and rock bridge going up to the barn floor. The first level of the barn was at ground level and was used to house the horses and cattle. A hayfork, of various designs, was stuck and/or hooked into the hay in the wagon to move it to the hay mow. The hayfork lifted the hay vertically to the top of the barn and then moved it along a horizontal track into the mow. The hoisting and moving was done by a system of pulleys. The hay was tripped off the hayfork by a trip rope when the hay was in the correct position.

Someone usually drove or led the horse. However, a well-trained horse could be used with only verbal commands from the man operating the hayfork. The horse would be started and when it had gone as far as necessary, the man on the wagon would yell, "Whoa." The horse would stop, turn around, return to the barn and again turn around, ready for the next hayfork load. The horse was trained not to step on the rope because its steel shoes could damage the rope, possibly causing an accident on later lifts. A wagon could be unloaded with about six lifts, depending on the hay stalk size, condition of the hay and the type of hayfork.

**Baling Hay**

Hay that was to be sold was baled prior to shipping in order to grossly decrease the volume. Hay baling was a dusty, dirty job, and clover was the worst of all types. The only protection that we had was long-sleeve shirts buttoned to the neck, bandannas tied around our necks and tied across our face, covering everything below our eyes. Long pants were worn to keep dirt out of our shoes and to protect our legs from scratches and insects. Nothing stopped the chiggers. My father got more than his share since he worked around the grain that had them every day in season. Mother would wash his back with soap and water, then with kerosene and after awhile with soap and water again. They attacked all parts of the body.

A steam engine or a tractor, the same as for the threshing machine, powered the hay baler. About nine men were required to efficiently work the hay baling operation. Four men worked out of the mow and up to the hay baler feeder table. The bales were removed from the baler discharge, weighed and stacked by two men. The custom baler used three men: one fed the baler; the second ran and hooked the baling wire; the third monitored and adjusted the machine and frequently hooked the bale ties for the man running the baling wire. The third man was usually the baling rig owner, and he frequently exchanged duties with the feeding man.

The length of the baling wire set the bale length and the bale weight was determined by how tightly the bales were packed. The bale density was controlled by an adjustment on the baler and was set at different tensions depending on the type and condition of the hay. Typical bale weights were eighty to one hundred pounds. A wooden built-up block was inserted between bales by the feeder operator as soon as the man running the baling wire yelled, "Block." If the block was put in too soon, the bale weighed less, and if it were inserted too late, the wires had to be spliced as they were too short to hook. The blocks had openings to run the baling wire through to the other side for hooking. If a block was improperly inserted the block may break and have to be replaced. My father made his own blocks and kept several on hand at all times.

Each bale was removed from the baler slide, weighed, and the weight marked on a wooden chip placed under one of three bale wires. Some operators only used two wires, but if one wire broke, unhooked, or slipped off, the bale fell apart. The small wood chips were made from cheese rings (boxes) obtained from the general store.

**Miscellaneous Farming Tasks**

The planting, growing and harvesting of these major crops were only a portion of the total farm work. Many other jobs had to be done routinely, both frequently and infrequently. Stock had to be fed and watered three times a day, as well as providing them with a clean, dry stable or pen. The horses and cattle were watered at the horse trough, which was located at the end of the wash house/spring house building. This was about two hundred yards from the barn and was connected by a lane about twenty feet wide.

A typical sequence of watering was to turn the horses out of the barn and they would go to the watering trough directly. They normally returned to their own stalls after they had drunk all the water they wanted. Grain was put in the feed trough, and hay in the hay rack, for each horse. These treats were incentive for the horses to return after drinking; otherwise, someone had to drive the horses back to the barn. Each horse was secured in the stall by a strap tied to the halter. At least a pole separated and formed the boundary of the stall. The harness was hung on the wall behind each horse for easy access.

Cattle were watered in a similar manner, except that each animal did not have a separate stall and none were tied. Hogs had both water and feed before them at all times, which were replenished at least once each day. Horses were fed corn, grain and hay, and the cattle were fed cracked or ground grain, cottonseed meal, ensilage and hay. The hay and ensilage provided filler having some food value.

There were several milk cows, which had to be milked twice a day, every day, at about six o'clock in the morning and six o'clock in the evening. During warm weather the cows were in the pasture field, which reached from the barn to the most remote point on the farm. However, they were trained to return to the barn for milking before six o'clock. The cows did not always promptly return, even though milking provided them with relief.

Most farmers had a trained stock dog to go out in the field and herd the cows to the barn. The dog was not always enthusiastic about the drive, and often refused to go when first directed. I remember seeing Aunt Mae pick old Jack up by his ears (shades of President Johnson!) and shake him to get him ready to make the drive. He would then go to the pasture field, round up the milk cows, and herd them to the barn for milking.

All milking was done by hand, for they had only two or three milk cows. Aunt Mae frequently did the milking and her accuracy was so good that she could squirt milk directly into a cat's open mouth! Each cow produced about two to three gallons of milk twice a day. The milk was strained and placed in a cream separator, and left there for six to twelve hours for the cream to rise to the top. Then the milk was drawn off at the bottom, and both the milk and cream were stored until used. Cream that was not used for cooking, coffee, cereal, etc., was churned into butter. Churning could take from twenty minutes to hours, depending on the cow, the cream temperature, churning rate, and the like.

The stables had to be cleaned and bedded with straw once or twice a day, depending on the animals and the weather conditions. Horses and cows usually sleep lying down, so that clean straw bedding was a necessity. The barn yard was cleaned once a year and the manure hauled to the field and spread using an aptly named machine called the "manure spreader." The manure was pitched onto the spreader using a pitchfork about eight inches wide and a foot long, with a straight, long handle.

The manure spreader was about twelve feet long, five feet wide, and two feet deep, and was pulled by two horses. A chain conveyer moved slowly to drag the manure to the rear, where the spreader blades tore up the manure and spread it evenly over the ground. The manure also contained straw from the bedding and corn stalks that the cows did not eat, all of which were beaten up and spread. I remember Mr. George Barb telling how Uncle John Myers gave him a straw fork (about twice the size of a pitchfork) and bragged about how much work George could do with it. George almost worked himself to death to live up to his expectation. Praise has always been a powerful tool.

Another farm job was keeping the fence rows clear of weeds, trees and vines, such as blackberry, poison ivy, and poison oak. The fence row was the area near the fence, which could not be farmed. The clearing was done using mowing scythes, grubbing hoes, axes, and just pulling out the weeds and vines by hand. I frequently worked in the poison ivy, since I was not allergic to it as many people were. The worst case of poison ivy I remember hearing about was that one or more persons got poison ivy in the lungs from having breathed in the smoke from burning dead ivy.

**Figure 6**
Arial View of Bowman Farm (The Old Martin Luther
Bowman & Ida Myers Bowman Home, Built 1918,)
Now Owned by Dick & Barbara Bowman

Chapter Five

# OUR HOMES

The homes of my grandparents as well as our two homes, which we lived in during the first sixteen years of my youth, are described below.

## My Parents' First Home

Mother and Dad set up housekeeping in 1920 in a home owned by Grandpa Bowman. It was located on three acres of land on what is now Route 614, about two tenths of a mile from Painter's Store. Grandpa Bowman had purchased this house from his brother in-law, John. The house was an "L" shaped frame house with four rooms downstairs and four rooms upstairs. The cellar had dirt walls and floor, and was under about one half of the house. There was a small back porch, and a front porch which ran the width of the house. A blue Concord grape arbor formed a canopy from the front porch to the yard fence along the road. Water was supplied from a cistern at the back end of the house.

Water for the cistern was supplied by run-off water from the house. This water ran down the gutters to down spouts directed to flow into the cistern. Both rain water and melted snow supplied the water. The drain spouts were turned off following rain or melted snow so that when the next rain or snow fell, it would not wash the dirt off the roof into the cistern. As soon as the roof was washed clean, the drain spouts were opened to let clean water flow into the cisterns. Cisterns were relatively small, therefore conservation of water was extremely important. As an example, wash water was saved and used to water the plants in the garden and the flowers in the yard.

The cistern was about sixteen feet deep and six or eight feet in diameter, with the sides relatively straight, but narrowing at the bottom. The top two feet of the cistern wall consisted of rocks stacked tightly together to support the wooden cistern top and keep animals out of the cistern. If an animal would fall into the cistern, it would drown and contaminate the water. The lower walls of the cistern were plastered with a thin coating of concrete to decrease leakage out of and into the cistern. It also helped prevent the dirt walls from deteriorating and falling into the cistern.

The cistern supplied water for cooking, for doing the wash, for cows, hogs and chickens, and for baths and washing one's face and hands. The cistern pump sat on top of and in the middle of the cistern top. The pump was a GEM pump, as most of them were in that area. The sheet metal pump casing was about three and half feet tall, six inches wide and fifteen inches long. The spout came out the side of the pump, and connected to a five inch by five inch by twelve inch reservoir within the pump casing.

A thin pipe about one and one half-inch in diameter was made into the bottom of the reservoir and extended to within about two feet of the bottom of the cistern. A cistern chain was threaded through the pipe, over the drive wheel and connected in an endless chain arrangement. The drive wheel was about twelve inches diameter, with forked prongs to grasp the chain, and was powered by a hand crank on the side of the pump near the top. The cistern chain consisted of links about two inches long with a sucker about every two or three feet.

The crank was turned clockwise, which pulled the chain up the pipe and through the reservoir. The suckers were flat round rubber disks, which fit snugly in the up pipe. These suckers pushed the water up the pipe into the reservoir, which then flowed out the spout to a bucket to be carried to its intended use. The cistern collected sediment in the bottom, and was cleaned when convenient. The cistern frequently went dry during long dry spells, and we took that opportunity to clean the cistern. The sides were scrubbed down and the water and sediment bucketed out using a rope and bucket. Water was then hauled from a well, town water, spring water, or anywhere else that good water was available, to tide us over until it rained.

There were also traveling cistern cleaners who came by and would contract to clean the cistern for about five dollars. Their cleaning rig consisted of a long pipe, and a bucket with a valve in the bottom and a closed top on the bucket. The empty bucket was pushed to the bottom of the cistern and pressed against the bottom. This opened the valve so that bottom water would rush into the bucket, carrying the sediment into the bucket. The bucket would be pulled up, dumped, and the operation repeated until little sediment came up in the bucket. The water was slightly stirred up and required a few days until the water was completely clear again.

The chain on the cistern pump could not be allowed to touch the bottom of the cistern or sediment would be stirred up each time water was pumped. This decreased the usable volume of the cistern by about five percent. The suckers had to be replaced, as they would wear and tear and not seal to the inside surface of the pipe. The chain links would also wear enough so that links would have to be removed to prevent the chain dragging on the bottom. If the links wore too much, they would break, and the chain would fall to the bottom of the cistern. The pump would have to be pulled out, the chain fished out with a long pole and hook, the chain repaired, and the chain restrung in the pump. The pump would then be reinstalled in the cistern. One knew when the suckers were wearing without looking at them, because then it would be necessary to pump faster to get equal flow. The suckers were replaced without removing the pump.

The house had a kitchen, dining room, living room and parlor downstairs, and four bedrooms upstairs. The house was heated downstairs with two wood or coal stoves. The stove pipes ran up through the floor and into the chimney upstairs. The stove pipe gave a little heat upstairs in two rooms. The house was partly log and covered with unpainted weather boarding. The front four rooms were log construction and the back rooms, added later, were frame construction.

There was also a combined wash house and smoke house, a barn with a garage, a chicken house, a hog pen, and a two-hole privy. There were two gardens and a pasture field with three pear trees. There was a "wet weather" spring in the pasture field, which provided water for the cows during wet seasons. No water flowed from the spring during dry weather.

After we moved out of this house, our Uncle Fred bought it. Uncle Roy and his family moved in and lived there for several years. The description above is how I remember Grandpa Bowman's house, my parent's first home, from my visits there with Uncle Roy. The monthly farm tenants and their families lived there after Uncle Roy's family moved. The house was sold by Uncle Fred many years ago.

## My Parents' Second Home : The Bowman Home

My parents bought about three acres of wooded land from Uncle John about a half mile up the road from Grandpa and Grandma Bowman's home. The Bowman land was bordered on the front by the state road, on one side by Mr. Ernest and Mrs. Lena Weatherholz's home, on one side by Mr. Green Clanahan's farm and on the fourth side by Salem Lutheran Church. They cut timber and used most of the lumber to build a house and out buildings. The house was completed in 1925, and we moved in later that year when I was an infant. The lumber was all oak, including the floors, doors, trim, sheeting, rafters, studs, and the like, and the support members were rough cut. The foundation was concrete. The outside of the house was weather board, painted white. The roof was tin, and the house had gutters all around to catch water for the cistern.

The home initially had no plumbing, only a pitcher pump in the kitchen with its suction in the cistern. The pitcher pump had an open discharge into whatever container you set under it. We used containers such as pans, dishes, washbasins, glasses, dishpans, cups, etc. A bucket of water was kept on the kitchen table to provide small quantities of water for drinking and cooking. The sink was about sixteen inches wide, thirty inches long and six inches deep and had no drain plug. It was used only to support the containers and let any spilled water discharge outdoors.

We took our baths using wash basins sitting in the sink or a small tub sitting on the kitchen floor. The "Saturday night bath" was a reality. Baths were normally taken on Saturday night with us boys taking ours and then going to bed. Our parents then bathed and went to bed.

The family installed indoor plumbing about 1948, six years after I left home. However, outdoor privy use was continued after indoor plumbing was installed to conserve water.

The house was "T" shaped, with the top of the "T" facing the road. The master carpenter was Mr. George Waterman. His helper was Mr. Eugene Lindamood. The trim was oak and finished like his father's house, but this carpenter made a different design with combing and graining.

There were four rooms downstairs, four rooms upstairs, with front and back stairs to the second story. There was a porch across the front of the house, which was about thirty feet from the road. The front door opened into a hall, which opened into the parlor on the left, the sitting room on the right, and the dining room at the end of the hall. The front stairs to the second floor were just to the left, and ahead as you entered the front door.

The kitchen was at the rear of the house on the first floor. The dining room was next to the kitchen, and the other side of the dining room opened into the sitting room. The parlor was across the hall from the sitting room, and was seldom used. A pantry opened off the kitchen at the end of the back porch. The back porch was screened on the side that was open. The back porch was used as the normal entrance and it opened into both the kitchen and the dining room. The back steps went from the kitchen to the back bedroom, which was my parents' bedroom.

The cellar steps were located under the back half of the house and connected the kitchen and cellar. The cellar walls were concrete and the floor was clay. Boards were placed on the dirt floor in the areas most often traveled, which resulted in less than ten percent of the floor covered. A drain was later added to carry away any water that leaked into the cellar in wet weather. There was a crawl space underneath the front part of the house from the cellar area.

A second set of concrete steps led from the back porch to the cellar. A large door, which was part of the porch floor, was raised to enter the cellar from the porch. This was opened only on special occasions, such as when potatoes, apples and meat were carried to the cellar for storage.

The cellar was used as food storage for items such as potatoes, apples, pork, vinegar, eggs, canned vegetables, canned fruit, sauerkraut, pumpkins and pickles. There were five shelves along one side for storage of the canned goods. Potato bins were along part of the other side and across the back. Our pork was hung on wires from overhead to lessen the chance of damage from mice. There was never a time that the mousetraps were not set, for this was a continual battle. We kept the vinegar barrel under the steps leading up to the kitchen.

Our kitchen equipment consisted of a "Lorain" wood cook stove, which was used to heat the kitchen and part of the dining room, cook the food, heat water for baths, cooking and to heat the flat irons for ironing clothes. The fire box was on the left end, the oven in the middle, the water tank on the right, and a warming closet about two feet above the cooking surface. The cooking surface was over the fire box and the oven and had removable covers over the various size holes. Certain kettles and skillets were made to set in the holes, and be directly in contact with the fire for greater heat.

My mother was usually the first one up in the morning, and she made the kitchen stove fire, as it could not be banked overnight. She kept corn cobs, kindling wood and a gallon can of coal oil (kerosene) at the end of the stove. The corn cobs and kindling would be put in the fire box and coal oil poured over it, and then lighted with a match. The matches were phosphorous-tipped and could be struck on any surface that offered friction. The matches were kept in the press (cabinet) near the stove in a match holder from "Robinson Produce."

The stove was supported on four legs with the bottom being about seven inches off the floor. Our fox terrier, Peggy, would lie under the stove day and night. She would get very hot under the stove when Mother was canning in the summer. She would then go across the kitchen, cool off, and go right back under the stove. I am not sure she was the smartest dog that ever lived!

The kitchen had about five chairs with one of them being an armless rocker. The kitchen table was across the room from the stove, and alongside the table was the pitcher pump and sink. The kitchen sink was used to hold two wash pans to use in washing our hands and faces. The pantry joined the kitchen via a door near the pitcher pump. The pantry contained cooking accessories such as crocks, flour, pie safe, coal oil lamps, cream separator in winter, slop bucket (for the hogs), cake pans, etc.

The dining room joined the kitchen and living room, and we kept the door open most of the time. The furniture in the dining room consisted of a dining room table, eight dining room chairs, buffet, the foot treadle New Home sewing machine, a bookcase, a radio and a rocker. We sometimes had a small wood stove in the dining room, which used the same chimney as the kitchen stove.

The living room had a relatively large coal-burning stove for heating that room and the dining room. We kept sweet potatoes and pumpkins as well as coats and hats in the living room closet. There was a day bed, which was used as a sofa, three rockers, three straight chairs and a roll top desk. My father kept his business records in the desk and his adding machine sat on top of the desk when not in use. This was a mechanical adding machine that weighed about forty pounds and was about eighteen inches deep, twelve inches wide and twelve inches high.

Our first living room stove was a cylindrical stove about eighteen inches in diameter. A cast iron bowl at the bottom of the cylinder contained the fire. The bowl would get red hot so it had a guardrail on each side to decrease the chances of someone getting burned. These bowls cracked after thermocycling many times and had to be replaced. Any good hardware store stocked the bowls. We roasted our feet close to the stove before going to bed in cold weather. This stove was replaced with a similar stove except it was inside a sheet metal shell. It was much larger than the first one but the heat output was about the same. It was not as good for roasting the feet.

Our home was furnished with very modest furniture. We had a few old pieces but essentially nothing was considered an antique at the time, although some pieces may now be considered antique, as 75 years does make a difference. Three of the four bedrooms had one double bed in each, and one bedroom had a double bed and a single bed. We three boys slept in the room with the two beds. The bedrooms were used only for sleeping and changing clothes.

Mother and Dad slept in the room that was the farthest from the road and nearest to the out buildings. This location gave them the greatest vantage point to hear the animals and chickens if either carnivorous animals or thieves disturbed them.

The house had an open-type attic with the height at the cone of the roof about four feet--a real head-knocker! The stairs to the attic became a storage area for Christmas decorations, things seldom used and items we just did not want to throw away. This was part of my basic "packrat" training.

The cistern was more refined and larger than the one at our first home. This cistern was about twenty feet deep and much of it had to be blasted out of limestone rock. The cistern top was concrete as well as the cistern walls and top support; therefore, no animals and only a little dirt could get into the cistern. The cistern was supplied by rain water and water from melting snow from the house roof and wash house roof. The cistern had an overflow about two feet from the top. I never knew why the overflow was not close to the top, say six inches. The chain and sucker pump was also a "GEM."

The combined wash house, smoke house and shop was a single two-story building located on the opposite side of the cistern from the house. The construction was frame and the sides were covered with galvanized sheet steel vaguely resembling bricks. The side sheets were nailed to oak sheating. The first floor consisted of two rooms with steps going to the shop on the second floor. The downstairs front area was the wash house and the other room the smoke house. The wash house contained a kettle stove for heating wash water and wash tubs and benches.

We bought a "Voss" wringer washer with two tubs about three years after we got electricity in 1934. The washing machine was a close-out at half price of forty dollars. My father was showing a neighbor how it worked, and being in the thick of things, I got my hand caught in the wringer and it ran up close to my elbow. Fortunately, it had the new softer rollers and was equipped with an emergency tripper bar, which my father quickly triggered. I was much more scared than hurt.

The smoke house contained shelves for sugar-curing the meat and hooks to hang the meat up for smoke-curing. This room was also used to store apples during the fall and winter months. The upstairs was used as a work shop, mostly for woodworking. The equipment consisted of the "horse head," work bench and hand tools. The horse head was used to hold the wood while it was shaved into useful items, such as ax handles, using a draw knife. The draw knife did not give a smooth surface and sand paper was expensive. We used broken glass to shave the wood to a smooth surface.

Surfaces that needed to be especially smooth were ball bats and tool handles for shovels, hoes and axes. The glass did a first class job. The attic space of this building was used to store scrap lumber. Dad did some machine repair work in this shop. The walls of the wash house and shop, as well as the floor areas of the shop, were used to store those treasures we could not throw away. This also added to my "packrat" training.

A two-car garage was built onto the back of the wash house about 1938. A coal bin extended half the length of the garage and about five feet wide. We were now a two-car family, a Model A Ford, and a 1937 Dodge, which was bought new. Anytime anyone bought a new car, all the neighbors came by to look at it and comment. The garage floor was dirt with a thin layer of gravel over the dirt. A second cistern was dug just behind the coal bin to increase the water storage. The garage water run-off was drained into this cistern. Additional piping was installed so that water from the house and wash house could be directed to this second cistern.

The barn was a two-story building constructed and covered the same as the wash house. The bottom of the barn had a cow stable for two cows and a concrete-floored hog pen for three hogs at one end. The other end was the garage for the Model A Ford until we built the two-car garage. That end was then used for a second cow stable and feed storage for the stock and chickens. A feed room was located between the two end units and used to feed the cows and slop the hogs. The upstairs was reached by climbing up a permanent ladder. Hay and straw were stored on this second floor and also some unused lumber, including cedar.

There was a small chicken house next to the barn, and as a part of the building, a two-hole privy. The privy was equipped with toilet paper (but no corn cobs), and catalogues--both Sears Roebuck and Montgomery Ward. This was one of the few "condo privies" in the community. We gave it this name, since this was built into the end of a chicken house instead of a free-standing building.

A round brooder house for small chickens was built using the same construction as building a wooden silo. The vertical tongue-and-groove two-inch thick boards were held together with 5/8" diameter steel hoops. My father later dragged the brooder house to another location using his Hart Parr tractor. The chief advantage of a round brooder house was that there were no corners in the building; baby chicks tend to huddle together in corners, and frequently some will suffocate. Perhaps the old statement, "Head for the round house Nellie, he can't corner you there," inspired this construction. A larger chicken house was built to house laying hens. The eggs were either sold for food or to the hatcheries for incubation.

The house and other buildings were all framed using rough-cut oak studs and boards and roofed with galvanized tin. The sheating was also oak boards covering the outside of the studs at a forty-five degree angle. Tar paper was put over the sheating and around the windows prior to the weatherboarding. The tar paper barrier was somewhat new, and the carpenters told Mother and Dad that they would have to go outdoors to get fresh air if the windows and doors were closed.

The inside of the house was covered with plaster lathe and plaster. The lathe were about one fourth-inch thick, two inches wide and spaced about one half inch apart. Snow brakes were installed on both the house and wash house. Snow brakes were necessary so that ice and snow would not slide down the roof and damage the gutters. The snow brakes also kept the ice and snow on the roof so that it would melt and run into the cisterns.

The garden was about one third of an acre and bordered on the road, the church property, the chicken yard and the lawn. A small orchard was located behind the small chicken house with both apple and peach trees. The orchard really never amounted to much, so was sort of a lost cause. We planted sweet corn, beans and pumpkins in the orchard to better utilize the land. After the ears were picked, the corn stalks were cut, a few at a time, and fed to the cows and hogs. This is where I smoked my first two and only cigarettes. One cigarette made me dizzy and one made me sick, so I apparently decided that enough was enough, and never smoked another cigarette.

Some incidents stick in one's mind for no apparent reason, and this is one that my mother enjoyed telling about for years. One evening about dark, when my mother was closing up the chicken houses to keep weasels, opossums, foxes, etc. out during the night, she spotted a skunk shucking and eating an ear of corn in the sweet corn patch. She called to Alden to bring the shotgun and some shells so she could kill the skunk. Alden grabbed the shotgun and shells and ran toward my mother with me close on his heels. He tripped over a small chicken coop, and the shotgun came apart in three pieces! The skunk lived to see another day.

Mother and Dad lived in this home and both died there; my mother rather suddenly and my father after a long illness. My brothers and their wives looked after my parents day and night during their illnesses, especially during my father's lengthy illness. Lois, my wife, and I gave them a little help about every other weekend, but the bulk of the care was done by my brothers and their wives. Lois and I lived in Newport News, Virginia, 200 miles away, where I worked full time. Many neighbors and other family members also helped take care of my father.

My nephew, Dick's son Philip Bowman, and his family have been living in this home for many years, and have added to and modernized it.

## Grandmother Dellinger's Homes

My Grandmother Dellinger's first home burned and she had to build a new home, which she built on a different site from her original home. The second house was built on about twenty acres of rectangular-shaped land, with the long side of the land bordering a public dirt road. A creek flowed across the land, creating a fourteen and six acre split. The house was located about one hundred feet from the creek and ten feet above it in elevation. The creek would overflow its banks during heavy rains, and the water would cover the entire lower yard. The lower yard was level and extended about seventy feet from the creek and about three feet above the normal creek level. The house was about ten feet above the level of the creek.

The slope of the hill was such that there was about six feet difference in elevation from one side of the house to the other. The house was a two-story rectangular-shaped building with the long dimension running along the hill. There was a small dirt cellar under part of it, which was used for food storage. The only entrance to the cellar was under the porch facing the creek. The porch had about a five-foot clearance and was closed in with latticework. This space under the porch was used as storage for items such as broken old chairs and old tools. The porch reached about the full length of the house, with steps at each end to the yard.

The house had six rooms, three upstairs and three downstairs, with seven-foot ceilings. The downstairs rooms were the kitchen, middle room and parlor. The kitchen had a pantry, a Lorain cook stove, an ice box, dining table with a bench between the table and wall, straight chairs and my Grandma's rocker. It was also used as the living room. The middle room had a cot-type bed, a single bed, straight chairs and a rocker or two. This room was used as another living room when needed. The parlor had a foot-pumped organ, an uncomfortable sofa and miscellaneous chairs and a small table.

The three rooms upstairs were all bedrooms. One guest bedroom had a double bed, table, chairs and mementos of family members. The center bedroom had two double beds, one for my grandmother and one for Aunt Polly. The third bedroom had a double and a single bed, and a walk-in closet. This was the only clothes closet in the house.

My grandmother and Aunt Polly slept on straw ticks. The straw tick was the same size as the bed, and about six inches thick. The straw was put in an inner tick cover that was put in an outer tick cover. We would help them replace the straw when we went to visit them. The straw was brittle and after a time it would break up into small pieces and be much less comfortable. We would get the straw from Uncle Bob's straw rick, being careful to get clean straw with no chaff.

There was a porch on the upper side of the house extending about two-thirds the length of the house. The usual entrance to the house was from the porch. A long grape arbor for Concord grapes was located between the house and the chicken yard, and these Concord grapes were especially good. The cistern was at the end of the upper porch away from the road. The summer kitchen was located about twelve feet from the end of the house. This kitchen was about twenty feet square and contained a Robert E. Lee cook stove, table and chairs, a bench, a wood box and a cupboard in one corner. The bench held the wash pans and soap as well as the drinking water bucket.

The summer kitchen was used only during the hot months of the year. The purpose was to cook in the summer kitchen, carry the food to the house and eat in the house kitchen. This kept the house cooler. The house kitchen was used in the colder months when the stove used to cook the food could also be used to heat the house. Wood was the fuel used and it was chopped and carried into the house by my grandmother.

The chicken house was up the hill above the house. The garden was between the chicken house and the other side of the land. The garden was very rich and the dirt was always loose, even during dry weather. The very bottom of the garden would get flooded during high waters.

Floodgates were provided across the creek at both sides of the land. The floodgates consisted of about eight-foot sections of wooden board fence held upright by a steel cable secured at each end and reaching across the creek. The weight of these sections prevented animals from pushing them aside and getting through. High water would float the sections so that the bottoms of the sections would be displaced downstream, and the water would flow under the gate sections. The gate sections would fall back into place as the water receded.

There was a smokehouse just beyond the summer kitchen and located at the edge of the garden. Garden and lawn tools were kept in the building along with other maintenance tools. The two-hole privy was located just inside the garden gates. This was one of the Roosevelt Public Works Authority privies. Uncle Wib commented during the Roosevelt-Landon 1936 election that Landon should run on the platform that he would paint the Roosevelt privies! There was a small barn up on the hill beyond the chicken house and a four-acre level field beyond the barn.

Grandma Dellinger sold the fourteen acres across the creek to Uncle Harold during the early 1930s. Grandma Dellinger and Aunt Polly died of rabbit fever (tularemia) in this home. My mother then bought the home from the other heirs, and she and my father maintained the house and yard for many years, letting relatives live in it. My mother later sold the property, and it has changed hands two or three times since then.

**Grandpa And Grandma Bowman's Home :**
**The Bowman Farm**

Grandpa and Grandma Bowman's house, built in 1918, was located on a one hundred-acre farm about one half mile from both our first and second homes. Grandpa Bowman had bought this farm from his parents' estate in 1912 at auction and then built a home there. The back side of the farm bordered on a gravel road and an entrance was available there but seldom used. The normal entrance was off what is now Route 614 down a half-mile lane to the house. The farm actually started about one thousand feet from the road with a right of way through Uncle John's farm to the corner of their farm. The total distance from the road to the house was about one half mile of private road, owned and kept up by my grandparents. The house was near one edge of the farm.

The front of the Bowman house faced the lane, but this entrance was seldom used. The family, the help and company used the side entrance to the kitchen and the living room.

At the end of the lane was a three-car garage, then a chicken house on the left, next the hog pen, a spring and a small holding pond on the right. Parking was on a large limestone rock, just outside the lower yard and spring house. This spring house was square with a tin roof and latticework on all sides and one door. It had benches around three sides to sit on to enjoy the cool spring water. The hired farm help frequently brought their lunches and this is where they sat to eat and rest at the noon hour. The pay was about one dollar and a quarter a day, if you carried your lunch, and one dollar a day if you ate with the family.

The tile casing to the spring was about two feet in diameter and six feet deep. The drain was about fifteen inches from the top and was directed to the trough in the spring house. The spring house was located in one end of the washhouse. It consisted of a concrete trough about two feet wide and of varying depths. Various containers were kept in this trough, such as thirty-inch high milk cans, crocks that were about twelve inches high, and other containers that may be less than six inches high. The water was about sixty degrees in the summertime.

The other end of the washhouse had a large fireplace as well as washing equipment such as washing machines, tubs and a wood-burning kettle stove to heat the water. The single cylinder gasoline engine drove the centrifugal cream separator for instant separation of the cream from the milk. As I remember it, they always spent more time getting the engine running than they spent on the separation process. There was also a grindstone driven by this same engine, which was used to sharpen tools such as mower blades, scythe blades, hoes and axes.

The upstairs was used as a storage area. The family lived in the wash house while they were building the family house. This was a log house covered with unpainted weather boards that looked to me like they could fall off at any time. Bats nested between the weather boards and the log wall. Dick and I would occasionally lay siege to the bats. Uncle Harry gave us an old tennis racket with no strings, so we covered the racket with a piece of tin. One of us would shake the boards and the other would swat at the bats as they flew out. We were exterminating unwanted pests and having great fun at the same time.

The horse trough was located outside at the spring house end of the building. This water was supplied from a spring located in the lower yard about thirty feet from the horse trough. The horses and cattle drank from the trough that was about twenty feet long, two feet wide and two feet deep. We children would lie down in this trough on very hot days, but not for long, since the water was some kind of cold right out of the spring.

The house was of construction similar to my parents' second home, with the same number of rooms, but the rooms were larger. The master carpenter was Mr. Issac Hite and his helper was Mr. George Waterman. Mr. Hite trimmed the house in oak and finished the doors with a combing and graining design. The cellar was under the kitchen and living room, and had concrete floor and walls. There was a spring under the house with a two-foot diameter casing and an overflow. The kitchen pitcher pump was connected to this spring for water used in the kitchen or from the small cistern under the porch. There was another smaller cellar to store some items such as the vinegar barrels and potatoes. A bathroom was installed during the mid-thirties, and an electric pump was connected to the spring to supply water to the house.

The kitchen was large and contained the dining room table as well as the stove and work table. A Philco radio sat on the kitchen table. The pantry was located off the kitchen and used for storage, and cabinets were installed in the wall next to the stove. The cabinets were mostly for storing dishes and cooking utensils and opened into both the kitchen and living room. The wood "Loraine" stove was replaced with a combination of wood and electric stove. The electric stove was used in the summer and the wood stove portion was used in the winter to help heat the kitchen.

The living room had a stove, living room furniture, my grandfather's rolltop desk, and the telephone. The furniture consisted of a sofa, a cot, easy chair, rocking and straight-back chairs.

The telephone number was 32-F-22. The 32 was the party line and the 22 was their ring designation. The 22 meant two shorts and two longs. An incoming call would be two short rings followed by two long rings, and this would be repeated until someone answered or the caller gave up. This party line must have had about fifteen houses on it and, of course, anyone could listen in as the 22 rang on their phones also. This was a one-wire line with conduction through the ground as one conductor and the other conductor was a bare wire on insulators. If too many phones were off the hooks to listen in, the sound could be so low that you could not hear or be heard. The ringing to call someone was by a hand-cranked magneto and the party number was rung by the short and long bursts of cranking the magnetos. The telephone line was repaired by the people served by the line. This repair included new telephone poles, repair of wire, replacement of insulators, etc.

The phone was also hazardous, in addition to being the telephone news distribution system. Balls of fire would come out of the telephone and go across the room during severe thunderstorms! Consequently, the living room was abandoned during storms but the door left open so they could be alert to fire. I never saw the phenomenon, but I never doubted it, as this telephone was on a stem line about one half mile long. High standing electrical waves could exist due to the antenna effect. I put in an extensive ground system for the telephone and electric service, which helped decrease the lightning strikes. The lightning would run into the bathroom, leaving burn marks and burning the bathtub stopper chain off. This phenomenon is still occurring in this house.

The parlor was the third room on the first floor, and contained an upright player piano as well as sofa and chairs. They had approximately one hundred rolls of music. We usually ended up playing this piano every time we went to visit at night. They had pieces of music such as "Under the Double Eagle," "How Dry I Am," and "The Old Rugged Cross." The fourth room on the first floor was used as a bedroom. All four rooms on the second floor were bedrooms. The attic was open construction and used for general storage from Christmas decorations to old rifles and new horse harnesses.

The house had four porches, three downstairs and one upstairs. The front porch, located on the front of the house, had a concrete floor and was seldom used. There was a second porch off the kitchen that faced the spring house. They screened it in so that my grandmother could stay there from the time she was diagnosed as having tuberculosis until she died. The third porch was located in back of the house, was also screened in, and served as the dining area during the warm months. It had roll down-roll up awnings to keep the rain from blowing in on the dining table. The porch had a large area holding up to fifteen people where threshing and silo filing hands ate. There was a fourth porch upstairs which was used for nothing that I can remember. Dad slept on this porch one winter, I guess just to show how tough he was.

The wood shed and smoke house were in one building and had a second floor over the smokehouse. This second floor was for storage such as beds, tables, chairs and even two swords. The wood shed was the larger part of the building. There was a spring behind this building, close to a chicken house.

There was an old "shanty" just beyond the chicken house, which was used to store chicken feed. The shanty's original use was to house the sawmill workers at the sawmill site during the week, because they did not go home except on weekends. It had fold-down tables, some kind of bunk arrangement, and was mounted on four spoked steel wheels and pulled by horses from sawmill site to sawmill site.

The barn, built in 1866, was constructed using hand-hewed timbers for the main strength members and sawed lumber for the studs, siding, walls and floors. The main strength members were fastened together with wooden pins, whereas the rest of the structure was nailed together. The barn floor was about ten feet above ground level. The area under the barn floor was used to house the horses, milk cows and beef cattle.

The stables ran perpendicular to the length of the barn. The overshoot of the barn was an area the length of the barn that opened into the stables. Animals could be taken from one stable to another in this overshoot area without exposure to the weather. Feed rooms were located between pairs of stables to feed the animals grain in the troughs and hay in the hay racks. The stables were cleaned by hand and the manure and soiled bedding pitched out into the barnyard.

A rock and dirt barn bridge was built on the side of the barn opposite the barnyard so that the wagons and other machinery such as threshers could be moved to the barn floor. Slate rock was frequently used in this fill as it compacted with use but may become slippery when wet, therefore other gravel was also used to reduce this hazard. The slope was about one in ten. The barn bridge permitted access to the center of the barn floor. A hay mow was located at each end of the barn. The hay was off-loaded from the wagons using a hay fork pulled by a horse. A silo was located next to the barn and barn bridge and opened into the lower level feed room. The ensilage was pitched down the chute to the feed room, where it was carried to the stock.

There was another chicken house and machine shed near the barn. The machine shed was used to store the machinery anytime it was not in use. Many farmers let their machinery sit outside, which caused it to rust and deteriorate, but not at this farm. There were four fields used to grow crops and one large pasture field. The crop fields averaged about fifteen acres each and the pasture field was about thirty acres. The remaining ten acres was for the house, yard, barn, orchard, lane and special uses. The rock, described under "Play" was located in the painter field, which got its name because it bordered on the Painter farm. There was a trash pile on a large rock near this chicken house that contained many, many items fascinating to young boys. We frequently spent time in the junk pile to see if there was something we could use.

**Figure 7**
Our Family Home (The Joseph Earl Bowman Home Built 1925), Now owned by Phillip Bowman and Family

**Figure 8**
Grandmother Dellinger's Second Home

**Figure 9**
Grandfather & Grandmother Bowman's Home, Built 1918 (Now Owned by Dick and Barbara Bowman)

Chapter Six

# FOOD

We grew just about everything we ate; we purchased very little from the grocery store. However, certain items could not be obtained in any other way, such as sugar, salt, coffee, tea, pepper and cereals like oatmeal and corn flakes. Sugar was the largest single staple and this was bought in one hundred-pound bags. We put it into old lard firkins stored on the step leading to the attic. The metal cans kept the mice from getting to the sugar. Sugar was scooped from these cans into an old 1 ½ gallon metal coffee can which was, of course, kept in the kitchen.

We grew some fruits, such as apples, pears, peaches, cherries and damsons, in small quantities or purchased them from the larger orchards. Vegetables were all grown in our one garden, which was a little more than one-third acre bordered by the road, the Lutheran Church property, our chicken yard and our lawn. A few vegetables, such as tomatoes and cucumbers, were moved each year but the other vegetables were planted at the same spot in our garden, year after year. We also maintained cows for milking and pigs to slaughter for food.

**Our Garden**

We produced most of our own vegetables in our own garden, which was about 150 feet long and 110 feet wide. We fertilized it during the fall by covering it with chicken manure from the chicken roosts, rather than using the chicken litter on the chicken house floor. The chicken manure had no straw, wood shavings or anything else in it, although feathers were always present. The garden was covered heavily with barnyard manure just prior to plowing in the spring. No artificial fertilizer was ever used in the garden.

We plowed the garden using a two-horse single-turning plow that turned a furrow about eight inches deep and ten inches wide. One year the garden was ploughed "haw," that is, the plowing would start at the garden's outside edge. This moved all of the ground ten inches from the inside of the garden, which left a low spot at the center of the garden. The next year the garden was plowed "gee" whereby the plowing started at the center of the garden, moving the ground ten inches toward the center. This plowing technique kept the garden relatively level. The garden was plowed along all four sides, not just from end to end. The rows ran the short dimension of the garden, 110 feet.

One major food staple our garden produced was potatoes. We usually planted Irish Cobbler potatoes, but now and then planted others such as Red Bliss, a choice which may have been related to the cost of the seed potatoes, or that a neighbor had such a good crop of a different potato the previous year.

Potatoes were cut into several pieces, with each piece containing one or two eyes. Each eye produced a potato stalk. If the seed potatoes were large, the centers of the potatoes were saved and eaten. The potato slices were rolled in sulfur and placed in the bottom of the row with the eyes up. If the eyes were down, the stalk would have to turn around thus growing further before breaking the surface (this may be an "old wives' tale"). Dirt was then put over the potato slices, which not only covered the potatoes, but also leveled the ground for easier cultivation after the potato stalks appeared above ground.

We usually planted potatoes the same day we plowed the garden so that we could use an available horse to lay out the rows and cover the dropped potato slices. We planted about twelve rows of potatoes about six inches deep, starting at the side of the garden away from the road. Some neighbors thought this was too deep, but the potatoes always came up.

Once the potato plants came up, they needed to be cultivated and weeded two to six times before they would fall over.

To kill potato bugs, we dusted the potato stalks with a powdered mixture applied while dew was on the stalks, by putting the powder in a sock or cloth bag and shaking it over each stalk. Frequently, we would manually pick the potato bugs off the stalks and put them in a tin can partially filled with coal oil (kerosene). This was slow and backbreaking work and was usually done by children because a child did not have to bend over as far as an adult, and besides, the adults had a multitude of other things to do. At least, that is what our parents told us.

We harvested our potatoes when their stalks were just about dead and the potatoes full grown. As soon as the potatoes were big enough to eat, we would "gravell" (dig the potatoes but not the potato stalk) enough of the potatoes for a meal or two. This continued until it was time to dig all the potatoes.

Some people dug the potatoes by hand, but we plowed ours out. We used a single shovel plow that my father made. The plow shovel was about twelve inches wide and twelve inches long, with a rounded but sharp end at the bottom. This was pulled by one horse, which had to walk slowly so the person guiding the plow could keep in the row. If he did not keep in the row or plowed too shallow, he would cut some of the potatoes. These cut potatoes were kept separate, washed and eaten before the others so that they would not rot.

One of the horses we used was "Nance," owned by my grandmother. This big gray mare was one of the fastest walking horses I have ever seen. My father operated the plow, and I remember one year when I was about ten years old, I was to lead and control Nance. She was so headstrong she could not be led while keeping her pace down. I walked backward in front of her with a thumb in the ring on each end of the bit to hold her back. It worked!

The potatoes were picked up, the dirt rubbed off of them, and then they were spread out in the yard to dry, preferably in the shade so that they would not sunburn. I think there were times in which we washed the potatoes before laying them out to dry. They were then put in the cellar for storage and preservation. Our potato bins were about four feet long, four feet wide and ten inches deep. The normal yield was about 20 bushels, which would supply us with potatoes until the next summer.

Potatoes would sprout in the cellar storage and the larger the sprouts grew, the more food value it took from the potatoes. So several times a year, we would have to break the sprout off of every single one of them. Even with care, the potatoes were pretty well shriveled up by summer, and new potatoes were a welcome sight. Many of our neighbors planted late potatoes but the early crop gave us sufficient potatoes for our use.

Two rows of "broom corn" were planted next to the potatoes. Broom corn was plowed and weeded several times during the season. When it was mature, the top of the stalk was cut off and carried under a pear tree in the yard. The seeds had to be removed from each straw before the broom straw could be made into brooms. This was done using a wash tub, a board and a dull knife or curry comb. The curry combs used were discards that had been used to curry the work horses. The board was put in the wash tub with one end against the bottom edge and the other end sticking out above the wash tub at an angle of about thirty to forty-five degrees. The stalk was laid on the board with the broom straws in the tub. Then the broom straws were stroked with a knife or curry comb until all of the seeds were removed. The broom straws were then put in small bundles and hung up to dry.

The dust or chaff from the broom corn operation caused the worker to itch so much that when he finished he took a bath even if wasn't Saturday! The stalks were taken to Mr. Will Estep, who made brooms for us, that we hoped would last a year. These were the only brooms we had, and they were first used inside the house and later for other work such as cleaning the chicken houses. The broom handles were cleaned and kept so that they could be used on next year's brooms.

Seven rows of sweet corn were planted next to the broom corn. In addition to cultivation and weeding, suckers had to be removed several times during the growing season to produce larger ears of corn. Corn was also sometimes sprayed or dusted to kill the corn worms that attack the ears. The corn ears were pulled when the corn silk started to turn brown, which gave the best corn-on-the-cob. Corn was planted at different times so that we could have fresh corn over a period of time. A few of the best ears were allowed to remain on the stalk to full maturity and these were used for seed corn the following year.

For the best and most tender corn on the cob, the corn was picked, shucked, silked, cooked and eaten in less than an hour. Much of the corn we produced was cut off the cob and canned for use during the year, but some was dried for later use. Infrequently, we would roast corn in the shucks, either over an open fire or in the oven. This helped retain the juices and flavor in the corn.

Beans and pumpkins were planted with the corn. The bean vines ran up the corn stalks so that bean poles did not have to be provided. The pumpkin vines ran on the ground in the corn patch. The corn stalks were cut and fed to the cows after the corn and beans were picked.

Thus the corn patch became the pumpkin patch from about mid-summer until the pumpkins were ripe. The pumpkins were gathered and stored in the cellar. Pumpkins of one type were large, some even weighing about fifty pounds, some of which were kept on the floor in the clothes closets.

Some pumpkins were made into pies and some were canned to be used for pies later. Mother usually made from six to ten pies at a time and a hot pumpkin pie was top drawer eating. Mother would often give us the first pie out of the oven. It would be too hot to eat, so we would set it on the cellar floor to cool more rapidly. As soon as it was cool enough, we'd begin to eat, and often we would eat the entire pie before we came up out of the cellar! We often put apple jelly on the pumpkin pies when they were served cold for dessert. Other jellies and preserves were also quite tasty.

Lima beans were planted in two rows next to the corn. These had to be staked so that the vines would be kept off the ground to prevent rot. There was a stake for each hill and four stakes were tied together at the top to make them sturdy, but this also made them more difficult to pick. The lima beans were picked and shelled, and most of them were canned to be eaten throughout the year, while we ate the fresh beans during the maturing time of the beans.

Sweet potato plants were sprouted in a hot bed. The hot bed was a wooden box with no bottom and placed about one foot deep into the ground. Whole sweet potatoes were put in the hot bed along with layers of horse manure. The horse manure produced the heat so the potatoes could start to sprout in the early spring months and be ready for planting when warm weather came. The box was covered during especially cold days and always at night to keep the small plants from freezing.

We planted three rows of sweet potato plants next to the lima beans on sweet potato ridges which were about eight inches from top to bottom. Little tilling was required because the vines soon covered the ridges and prevented weeds from growing. The ends of the vines on the outer two rows were either cut off or bent back to keep them from spreading to the adjacent plants. The vines were still green when the sweet potatoes matured, so they were fed to the cows. The sweet potatoes were usually dug up, but sometimes were plowed out, picked up, washed, dried and stored for use during the winter and spring.

Cucumbers were planted next to the sweet potatoes. These had to be tilled, weeded, vines folded back and sprayed or dusted for bugs. Cucumbers were eaten during the growing season and made into pickles and canned for use during the year. Some cucumbers were put in crocks and preserved with salt brine.

Cantaloupes were usually planted at the end of the cucumber patch, but they frequently failed because of dry weather. We had no water available to water the garden, but we hauled water from a nearby pond in old milk cans in our play express wagon when we set out plants such as sweet potatoes, cabbage and tomatoes.

The cabbage patch was next, with about four rows of cabbage, one early and three late. These required the usual tilling, weeding and dusting. Cabbage was cooked or made into cole slaw during the growing season. Cabbage heads were stored in the cellar for use during the late fall and winter to make sauerkraut. The cabbage was cut up and put in a large crock with a board weighted down by a limestone rock to keep it compressed. I never cared for sauerkraut, and I think this was because of its appearance and smell while in the cellar. I ate it just the same, for that was the house rule: you eat some of everything.

Tomatoes were planted next to the cabbage, one row of early and four rows of late tomatoes. The late tomatoes were beefsteak tomatoes and much better and larger than the early tomatoes. The tomatoes were eaten as soon as the first ripened, about mid-July, until frost. The remaining green tomatoes were picked before the first frost and put in the cellar to ripen. We would have tomatoes until about Christmas, but they were not as good as vine ripened ones. They compared to those you get in the grocery store today when local tomatoes are not available.

My mother would make tomatoes into catsup and would also can enough tomatoes to fill the top shelf in the cellar, which held about 150 half-gallon jars. The amount she would can would depend on how many tomatoes we had and how many jars were left over from the previous year. We ate tomatoes for breakfast, dinner and supper when they were in season. Mother frequently fried green tomatoes for me.

Bunch beans were planted next to the tomatoes and bunch butter beans planted next to the bunch beans. These were eaten during the summer and canned for eating the rest of the year. These did not require poles, as they only grew twelve to eighteen inches high. Butterbeans as well as the lima beans were shelled before canning. Since beans all matured at the same time, they had to be picked and shelled within a few days. Mother and us boys picked them during the day and after supper the whole family sat on the screened-in back porch and shelled them. Mother canned them the next day.

Celery was another vegetable grown in the garden that required a lot of effort. The celery plants were first grown in a seed bed and then set out in two rows about ten inches apart and ten inches between plants in a given row. We started to ridge the celery stalks when they were about ten inches high. Ridging celery consisted of holding the stalk in a tight bundle and putting dirt around them so that the stalk would bleach. Newspapers were sometimes wrapped around the stalks before putting the dirt around them. This eliminated much of the dirt from being inside the stalks when they were dug up for eating. Ridging was repeated as the stalks grew until near frost.

Before frost, boards were put on either side of two celery rows and filled with dirt. Dirt was then piled four to six inches over the tops of the celery stalks to prevent the stalks from freezing. The stalks were brought into the house in small quantities, such as ten stalks at a time, and were put in the cellar on the damp dirt floor until they were eaten. Sometimes the dirt over the celery was covered with horse manure as the heat generated helped prevent freezing.

There was a great variety of small-quantity items planted in the remaining garden. These included strawberries, onions, leeks, salsify (also called "oyster plant" or "vegetable oyster"), parsnips, parsley, lettuce, carrots, peppers and radishes. The seed bed was also in this area to grow plants such as tomato, cabbage and celery. The early tomato and cabbage plants were grown in containers in the house so that they would be ready to set out as soon as the temperature was warm enough.

Mother also grew flowers and roses in the part of the garden that was near the road. The flowers were used for the house and to take to the cemetery in memory and honor of loved ones. I remember one time Mother set out tomato plants in a very crooked row. When my father commented on the crooked rows, my mother replied that she had done this so that the "cut worms" could not follow the row and cut down every plant! We also had a small quantity of popcorn that had to be kept as far away as practical from the sweet corn to prevent cross-pollination.

### Cows And Milking

We kept one or two milk cows to supply us with dairy products for personal consumption. The cows were usually Guernseys, Jerseys or a cross of the two. At one time we also had a black pole cow. The Guernsey gave the richest milk and the black pole the poorest. The cows were kept in the pasture field during the spring, summer and fall, and in the barn during winter. The pasture would not support two cows, so we would take them to pasture at my grandmother's farm during the day.

We would sometimes try to ride the cows to pasture, but as soon as we would get onto them they would run under a tree with low branches and scrape us off. There is absolutely nothing on a cow to hang onto. We never had any broken bones, but we frequently had scratches and bruises. This activity frequently could lead to a bit of switch discipline, for we were reminded the cows were producers and not toys. (The cows were also our pets but more about that under "Play.") We would brand the cows in spring by pulling out the loose winter hair in the shape of a cattle brand or frequently our initials. The markings disappeared as the winter hair was shed.

Our first cow was bought right after my mother and father set up housekeeping. They named her Rhoda, which I always thought was an ugly name. My parents sold her after using her to produce milk and calves for over fifteen years. If she was sold for beef, I bet that was one tough piece of beef. She was sold for one and a half dollars more than they had paid for her seventeen years earlier!

My mother did the milking most of the time. The cows were milked outdoors in warm weather and in the cow stable in cold weather. Some of the cows would not stand still outdoors and would have to be tied or held during milking. Dick and I helped by making the cow and mother more comfortable. One of us would continually brush the flies off the front legs and belly of the cow and the other one would hold the cow's tail so she would not switch her tail and beat mother in the head. The cows were kept in the barn and barn yard in the winter and fed hay and grain. They were also fed some grain in the summer in addition to grazing the pasture. The pasture furnished bulk and the grain furnished substance.

Milk was used for cooking, drinking and cereal, and the cream was separated leaving skimmed milk. Cream was used for cooking, coffee, over fruit pies and apple dumplings, ice cream, butter, and some was sold. Mother always made ice cream and cake for our birthdays and invited the neighbor children. The skimmed milk was used to make cottage cheese or fed to the hogs or chickens.

There was one day when all the family except my father had gone away. Milking was of special concern, since he never did any milking. When we came home that night, one of the first things my mother asked my father was, "How did the milking go?" My father replied, "Not so great," but he kept the cow from bursting. My mother looked at the milk bucket and said, "You have about as much hair as you do milk." Later on he asked mother about frying eggs. His question was, "Should the grease be boiling when you break the egg in the skillet?" Needless to say, he was seldom left to shift for himself.

**Meats and Pigs**

Occasionally we would buy beef, and a few times we bought a quarter of beef. We put some of it in a freezer at Mt. Jackson and my mother canned some of it. She had a special board and hammer for tenderizing the beef. Once in a while, Uncle Tom would give us some mutton. Alden did not like it, but Mother disguised it as beef and after Alden ate two pieces, he was told what it was. Mutton was all right after that. On one occasion Dad and some neighbors bought a keg of salt fish. The look and smell of this turned Dick against fish for several years, and no wonder.

Each November or December we would purchase two or three pigs to be raised and butchered the following year after cold weather commenced. If we purchased them later, we would have to buy shoats, which were larger than the pigs. The pigs were kept in the pig pen and were slopped (fed liquid and solid food) twice each day, morning and night. They were fed food waste such as tomatoes, potato peels, milk, etc., which was supplemented by grain or meal such as ground corn, bran and a special mix called middlins (a mixture of flour and bran) made up for hogs. The hog pen was both indoors and outdoors with a concrete floor. The inside was at least partially covered with straw for bedding.

We kept our pigs penned inside during the cold winter nights with plenty of bedding for them to sleep on. Fresh straw bedding was added each night after the pen was cleaned. The same care was given to the cows. The hogs were rung in the spring and turned out in the pasture with the cows. There were from four to six rings put in each pig's nose so that he could not root and tear up the field. When they tried to root, the rings would hurt their noses. Care had to be taken when ringing the hogs so that the rings would be effective and not harm the hogs. Rings could not be put in the center of the nose, as this could damage the hog's nerves and even kill the animal.

There were many ways of holding the hog to put the rings in its nose. If the animal was not too big, one person could hold it by the ears while a second person crimped the copper colored rings into place. Hogs would have to be rung more than once since they could wear or tear the rings out or would outgrow them. We held a larger hog with a slip wire loop over its mouth, which held the jaws closed. The hog would be backed up into a corner and held securely while the second person crimped the rings in place. This was not a fun job. The hogs squealed loudly and continuously.

The hogs also became pets of a sort during the summer, but we never really controlled them. We would hop on them and ride across the pasture field, or at least try to. A hog is a very difficult animal to stay astride of. Big Red was one of our favorites and as soon as one of us hopped on him, he would head for the sand brier patch to buck us off. These hogs may have been smarter than we were.

Hogs were put in the pen and fed grain, such as corn, to fatten them for the kill. Butchering day was after the warm days were gone and cool days had arrived. The meat was cured at room temperature, so the outside temperature and the unheated smoke house had to be cold enough to prevent spoilage.

Butchering day was a long day for grownups, but a fun day for children. The children did some tasks, but most tasks were for adults. I never remember any whimpering by us boys as we watched the hogs slaughtered. This was just the way it was and we knew it. Mother never came to the barn yard until after the hogs had been killed because she did not want to see the hogs being shot and stuck.

We usually had about four or five men and two or three women helping on butchering day. Mr. Foltz was in charge of the detail work and seeing that everything was done properly. He probably butchered for twenty families in the area each year. The hogs were brought out of the hog pen into the barnyard where they were shot with a .22 caliber rifle. They were immediately stuck through the throat and into the heart with a butcher knife so that most of the blood would flow from the animal. The dead hogs were moved to several positions to aid in the bleeding.

The outdoor butcher kettles were filled with water the night before and wood placed under the kettles to set on fire early in the morning. The fires were lighted by at least 5:00 a.m. so that the water would be hot before the animals were killed. The hot water was put in a scalding trough large enough to lay the hog in. The water temperature was extremely important so that the hog would be exposed to the proper temperature to aid in the hair removal.

The amount of time the hog was in the scalding trough was also important. The temperature of the water was about 160 degrees when the hog was rolled in. Each hog weighed about 250 to 300 pounds, so you see that you needed several strong men to get the hog into and out of the trough. The time in the trough was determined by scraping the hog hair to see if it came off easily. The hog was removed from the trough and the hair scraped off with hog scrapers as it lay on boards. The scrapers were a relatively thin circular metal with a wooden round handle. Some farmers scalded the hogs in a large barrel with one end of the barrel removed. The barrel was mounted at about a forty-five degree angle with the open end up.

The hog's hind legs were slit and the tendons pulled free so that they could be used to support the hog. The hog was hoisted up using a tripod butchering pole. These three poles were about twelve feet tall with a bolt at the top end holding the poles together. Each hind leg of the hog was fastened to one of the outside poles by a cylinder spike. The center pole was pivoted in the opposite direction of the outer poles. The bottom of the single pole was pushed toward the bottom of the two other poles, raising the hog off of the scalding trough boards. The poles were moved until the hog's nose was a few inches off the ground.

The hog was further cleaned by more scraping and washing with hot soapy water. The hog was shaved using soap, hot water and a sharp butcher knife to remove any hair not removed by the scraping. The next operation was cutting off the head and putting it, nose-up, on a head stake. The head stake was made of wood, such as a four by four, with the upper end sharpened to receive the head. One person frequently spent a good portion of the day dressing the heads, and of course he was the designated "head man."

The next step was to remove the hog's entrails. The hog was slit from the rear end to the front end on the belly underside. The entrails were rolled out of the hog into a wash tub and were taken to be processed, usually inside the wash house. The useful meat, such as the heart and liver, were removed for further use. Useless parts, such as the lungs, were either buried or thrown out for the buzzards. The small intestines were cleaned and used as casing for links sausage or puddins. The bladders were cleaned and filled with sausage for summer sausage.

The hanging hog then was spread open, washed and cleaned thoroughly. The tenderloin was removed and carried to the butcher table. The ribs were cut at the backbone using a very sharp ax. The backbone was then cut from the hog using butcher knives and carried to the butcher table.

There were then two pieces of meat with one hanging on each pole. Each piece consisted of one shoulder, one ham and side meat. These two pieces of meat would be carried to the butcher table when needed for processing. More than one hog was worked at the same time, the process controlled by the help and facilities available. The piece with the shoulder, ham and side meat was cut apart on the butcher table and each section was trimmed and carried to the smoke house for sugar curing. The trimmings were used for lard, sausage and puddins.

Fat meat was diced up into small one-inch cubes and used for lard. The fatter the hog, the more lard had to be rendered. The lard was cooked in an open kettle over an open fire until it was ready to be rendered. Cooking it too much would cause the lard to be dark and strong, both of which were undesirable. If it became too strong, either because of too much cooking or being stored too long, it was frequently used to make homemade soap. The cooked fat was put in a lard press, where the liquid would run through. This cooked fat was then pressed so that all the liquid would be squeezed out to solidify as lard. The lard press was hand cranked and the fat compressed to about one fourth of its cooked volume. The pressed fat solid was in a cake about eight inches diameter and three inches thick, and was called craklins. These were fed to the chickens. The lard ran into six-gallon cans called lard firkins and was taken out of the cans as used.

The lean meat trimmings were separated from the fat and mostly processed as sausage. This meat was cut into strips or small pieces and ground in the sausage grinder. The sausage grinder was usually hand cranked; however, the crank could be tied to the rear wheel of an automobile. The automobile would be run at idle speed with the transmission in low gear, and the car wheel jacked off the ground. This was really "living." Some of the lean meat may also be put in the puddins. The sausage stuffer was the same equipment as the lard press except that different parts were used in the cylinder. We stuffed sausages by hand cranking.

Puddin meat consisted entirely of lean meat, which was cooked until done in an open kettle over an open fire. Meat used for this included ham and shoulder trimmings, head meat, liver, heart and tongue. This was usually cooked enough to eat before noon, so our dinners (eaten about noon) were frequently ruined by too much puddin meat. The puddin meat was ground in the sausage grinder, which turned much easier than when grinding raw lean meat for sausage. The puddins were either stuffed in casings like sausage or canned for use throughout the year. Puddins were extremely good on hot cakes and even better when you put syrup on top.

The broth from the puddin meat was used to make "pon haus." Cornmeal, bits of meat in the broth, and other seasonings were added to the broth to make a thick slurry. This was cooked and then poured into bread pans and other pans to let cool and solidify. This was then sliced and fried in the skillet and served as an extra or in place of the meat. Fried pon haus with apple butter on homemade bread was one of our favorites. Pon haus was sometimes eaten without any further cooking.

The backbone was sawed up into two or three inch lengths. It contained considerable meat and served us many meals. The tenderloin was sliced and was used in our school lunch sandwich. We frequently asked Mother to get us bologna, as we were tired of ham, sausage, tenderloin, etc. Children are not always the brightest. We didn't realize what a delicacy we were eating until we left the farm!

Every bit of the head was used; the tongue, lean meat, ears and brains. We always looked forward to the day Mother fried the brains, for there was only enough for one meal and then we had to wait a year for another serving. The pig's feet and ears were cooked and souse was made of what was not eaten at the first cooking. Souse was not a favorite, but we ate it anyway.

The butchering was usually finished by four or five o'clock except for sugar curing the meat, cleaning up the equipment, and returning the borrowed equipment. No one had all the equipment needed, so families borrowed from each other. We usually borrowed the scalding trough, two kettles, the sausage grinder and the sausage stuffer. Everyone that helped was given a "mess" to take home. A mess frequently consisted of sausage, puddins, pon haus, and liver or tenderloin. You also took a mess to your nearby neighbors even if they did not help. The chief butcher was paid but most others were help-for-help-back.

The women were quite busy. One person was busy cleaning the sausage casings, which had to be done carefully or they may have holes in them or not be completely clean. One person prepared dinners and helped with many other jobs, such as stuffing the sausage and puddins. I have not mentioned everything that was done, such as preparing the sweetbread, because I do not remember all the details. Cider and coffee were served. The noon meal was similar to the thresh day dinner, but not as many people were involved. We would often invite relatives and friends in for puddin meat and/or butcher dinner.

My brothers and I enjoyed playing with the pig's tails. The object was to pin it to someone's coat tail and see how long it would be until he realized it. The outstanding pigtail story at our home was when Uncle Wib, with his great sense of humor and knack for tricks, did his thing. He cleaned the pig's tail extremely well and stuffed it in a sausage casing with the sausage. This sausage was part of his mess that he took home, but Aunt Stella knew nothing about it. The next morning Aunt Stella fixed this foot-long piece of sausage. When she put it on the table, Uncle Wib said he did not care for any. Aunt Stella cut off a piece of the sausage and saw the pig tail. She said, "I knew Earl Bowman was a dirty butcher, but I never thought he was this dirty!" I don't recall that anyone else ever topped this trick.

The shoulders, hams, side meat, summer sausages, etc., were sugar cured. Everyone had his own mix and I do not remember what ours was, but it surely gave the meat a good flavor. The sugar cure was thickly applied on the meat, maybe one-half inch. This drew out the blood and flavored the meat. After several weeks, the sugar cure was scraped off and the meat hung up in the smoke house. The meat was then hickory smoked for a day or two for the smoke to penetrate the meat. Each piece of meat was put in a cloth bag and hung in the cellar until used. The smoked sugar-cured ham was especially good when fried and even better when eaten raw near the bone. We were only allowed small slivers of the raw lean meat and were told that too much of this would give us worms. Enough said.

## Chickens and Eggs

We always had chickens of one kind or another and for specific purposes. Several kinds were Leghorns, Plymouth Rock, White Rock and Rhode Island Reds.

The chickens were either grown as broilers and sold, as layers and the eggs sold, or as layers and eggs sold to hatcheries. We always bought baby chickens from the hatchery regardless of their intended use. They came from the hatchery in cardboard boxes with four divisions of twenty-five chicks each, one hundred per box.

We normally bought no more than 500 chicks at a time and this was usually during cold weather. They were put in our brooder house, which was heated with a brooder stove. The stove was about three feet tall and not very large in diameter. The hard coal was put in the top with the fire in the bottom. The coal fed down to the fire as it burned. Ashes were removed from the bottom. There was a large sheet metal frustum of a cone shape that fitted over the stove called the hover. The hover was about six feet in diameter near the floor and the angle of the top of the cone frustum was about one hundred and twenty degrees. The outer lower diameter was about twelve inches off the floor, and much more than half of the heat was under the hover.

The baby chicks sat under the hover at night to keep warm and rest to promote growth. The chicks had to be trained to sit around and under the hover. This was done during the first week. Chickens, especially small chicks, tend to migrate to corners, where they tend to pile up. If they are allowed to pile up, some of them may smother. Our brooder house was made from old silo boards and held together with the same kinds of steel rod hoops. Of course, it was round, so there were no corners where the chicks could gather. During the training period, our technique was to chase the baby chicks around the brooder house with a broom, pushing them toward the stove. The idea was to have an equal density ring of chicks at the edge and/or under the hover. After they settled down they were good for the night unless they were spooked by an animal. During the first few nights with baby chicks, you actually almost "slept with the chickens" to be sure they did not pile up and suffocate.

The small chick feeders were placed between the stove and the wall and mash was kept in front of them at all times. Cracked grain was frequently given to them two or three times a day. Water was always before them. The containers for their food and water had to be constructed so that the chicks could eat and drink but not be able to sit in them. Since they did not know any better, they would mess up the food and water if they sat in the containers. This is true for all chickens regardless of their size. They just do not think far ahead, like the next meal! As the chicks got larger and full-feathered, the temperature was not so critical since feathers are good insulators. The chickens also outgrew the brooder house so that some of them had to be moved to another chicken house.

The broilers were grown to about two to three pounds in fifteen weeks. They now grow them to about five pounds in seven weeks, so this industry has made drastic changes. Broilers were usually sold to a huckster who took them to market, usually Washington, D.C. Some broilers were our Sunday dinner, but the best were sold. The chicks sat on chicken roosts after they were a few weeks old and this was also a training process. They would go to roost about or a little before dark, thus the "go to bed with the chickens" expression was born.

The roosters were always sold, but the pullets were frequently kept as layers. Of course roosters were needed on about a ten to one ratio to keep the hens happy. These roosters came from another flock, as incest was not permitted (morality in the chicken house!). Nests were provided for the hens to lay their eggs in, but there were always some that did not get the word and laid their eggs wherever the notion struck them. Their eggs were not all like the ones you see in the grocery store. About two percent were other than normal; the two most frequent varieties were double yolk and soft shells. The percentage of double yolks varied greatly from flock to flock, and I know of no way to eliminate the double yolks, so we just ate and enjoyed them. Soft shell eggs indicate improper diet, so the first thing to check would be whether ground oyster shells were available to the hens.

There were some other peculiar aberrations in eggs. We had one hen, or assumed it was only one, that laid about ten eggs, each weighing five to six ounces, which is three times the normal egg weight. This large egg had a yolk and white, but in addition had another completely formed normal egg inside the large outer shell! No one in the neighborhood knew of any other eggs like these.

The eggs that were sold to the hatchery required special attention. Blood was drawn from the underside of one wing of each chicken and sent to the laboratory for testing. This was done every six or twelve months, and no more than about two percent were allowed to fail this procedure, otherwise the whole flock had to be retested. The cost for testing each chicken was about eight to ten cents. Each chicken had an aluminum band with a unique number. Chicken thieves were not unusual, and we had some stolen. Leg bands from some of our stolen chickens were found back in the mountain ten to fifteen miles away. Sometimes owners would set shotguns rigged to go off when the chicken house was entered by someone not knowing how to disarm the weapon.

A chicken can be carefully picked up without a flutter or noise if you know how. We kept two to three hundred layers most of the time. The egg-laying career of chickens was about four years, and then the flock would have to be replaced.

## Nuts, Fruits, Berries and Melons

Black walnuts were the only nuts we processed for our own use. These were picked up under the walnut trees in the fall, brought home and spread out for partial drying. The walnut hulls were removed and the walnuts were again spread out to dry. Hulling walnuts was not a fun thing to do. The walnut was hit with a mallet to partially crush and crack the hull open. The hull was then removed by hand. It was always easy to see who had been hulling walnuts--their hands were brown for several weeks until the walnut stain wore off. The hulls could also be removed by running them through a hand operated corn sheller, but that was academic since we had no corn sheller.

We would crack the walnuts to get the kernels out for cookies, cakes, and simple eating. Dad cracked most of the walnuts that were used for cooking. Mother would crush the walnut kernels with the rolling pin and use them to make icing. The top of the cake and sometimes the sides were partially covered with the larger of the kernels. Walnut cake was one of the family's favorites.

We had one small sour cherry tree, but it never produced more than about a gallon or two of cherries that we used mostly for pies and cobblers. One day each summer we would pick cherries, usually sweet black cherries. Dad would help if it wasn't a good day for thrashing. He would take Mother and us boys to the cherry trees, where we would climb and pick from the tree, from a ladder and/or from the truck bed. We would sometimes pull the lower limbs down with a rope and tie the rope to the trunk of the tree. Then no climbing was necessary in order to pick.

We would pick from one to three bushels if they were available. Some of the cherries would be canned with the seeds in them, and others would be seeded. We would seed them by hand and also by using a small hand-cranked cherry seeder. The whole cherries would be eaten as dessert, served directly from the cans or in cherry pies and cobblers.

Another day was devoted to blackberry picking. Dad would take Mother, Dick and me by the blackberry field about six-thirty in the morning on his way to the thresher. We took lunch and water for the day, and frequently picked eight to twelve gallons of blackberries. Dad would pick us up after six o'clock that evening. Snakes, chiggers and blackberry thorns were the hazards of this job, and it made for a long, long day. Mother canned most of the blackberries for pies and cobblers.

We grew some apples and peaches in our small orchard, but these really did not amount to much. Most of the apples and peaches were bought from the professional orchards. We bought the peaches from orchards such as the Buck Hill orchard during August. The white peaches were better for eating. We usually bought about six bushels with no more than one bushel being the white ones. We ate many of these and others were sliced, sugared and served over cereal and over cake. One kind of the yellow peaches that I remember was the Alberta, and another was Clings. The Clings must have gotten the name from the way the fruit would cling to the pit. The Clings were not popular. Peaches were usually canned in half-gallon mason jars and kept in the top shelf in the cellar.

We also purchased fifteen to twenty bushels of apples each fall. We bought a few Delicious apples, but most of them were Staymans and Yorks. The Yorks kept the longest without rotting, but they did not taste as good as the Staymans. A portion of these apples were ground hogged—picked off the ground under the trees--and sold for only a fraction of picked apple price. These ground hogged apples were frequently riper, much more bruised and had many more blemishes than the apples picked from the trees. Ground hogged apples were usually eaten first and also used to make apple butter, apple jelly, cider and applesauce. We always bought tree-run apples because these had not been run over the graders and bruised. There were also various-sized apples for different uses. The orchards paid three or four cents per bushel for picking. A number of third and fourth year high school students dropped out of school four to six weeks to pick apples to help the family income.

We stored the apples we did not immediately use for availability during the winter and spring months. A few bushels were stored in bins in the cellar to be used during the late fall and early winter. Those to be used later were specially packed and stored. Each apple was wrapped in paper and placed in wood barrels that held two or three bushels. Magazines and newspapers were saved during the year and used for the wrappings. Individually wrapping each apple helped to prevent a rotten apple from causing nearby apples to rot earlier. We defied "one rotten apple spoils the barrel." The barrels were either stored in the smoke house or placed in the cellar. We had apples until late spring or early summer depending on how well the apples kept.

We bought a fifty-gallon barrel of cider every few years. What we did not drink in the fall or can for later in the year was made into vinegar. Some of the "Mother" was taken out of the active vinegar barrel and put in the cider barrel to start the chemical reaction. Cider was a popular drink especially when it got sharp. Shortly after it got sharp it turned to vinegar.

Watermelons and cantaloupe were bought from Lohrs near New Market. The watermelon and cantaloupe patch was on the river bottom land. I assume they used some kind of irrigation getting the water from the North Fork of the Shenandoah River. These melons were a real treat for the whole family. Two occasions are very vivid in my memory. The first was that Aunt Bertie and her date brought about six large watermelons by about midnight. My father got up to receive and pay for them. He also ate almost a half of one melon. The other time was when Dad left home one day and said nothing about where he was going. He bought eight watermelons and two packs of cigarettes and then went to the dentist and had all his teeth pulled! Mother was, to say the least, a bit shocked at the episode. He normally smoked a pipe, but he knew that he could not hold it with no teeth while he surely could at least eat watermelon!

**Sweets and Snacks**

In those days we ate only homemade sweets, such as cakes, cookies, pies, candy and popcorn balls. The most popular cakes were walnut, caramel, chocolate, devil's food, angel food, applesauce and "lightning" cakes. The walnut cakes were usually three or four layer cakes with plenty of icing. The icing was soft and was rich with crushed black walnut meat. Large pieces of walnut kernels were put on the top and sides of the cake for both looks and just plain good eating. The caramel and chocolate cakes were usually three layers with a generous covering of icing. The devil's food, angel food and applesauce cakes were made in rather large cake molds, about four inches high. Applesauce cake usually had black walnuts throughout and sometimes raisins.

"Lightning" cake got its name from the short time it took my mother to make it. It was served hot with hot sugar syrup generously poured over it.

Popular cookies were ginger cake, lemon crackers, oatmeal cookies, sugar cookies, and donuts. All were large cookies, about three eighths-inch thick and three inches in diameter. The ginger cake cookies were very gingery, while the sugar cookies were coated on top with sugar. Donuts were seldom made and were not as appetizing as the cookies.

We enjoyed a large variety of pies, such as apple, peach, cherry, blackberry, raspberry, chocolate, lemon, pumpkin, butterscotch, yes, and even rhubarb. We normally had only one kind of pie at a time, but my mother occasionally made up to eight pies at a single baking. Three boys could put away many a pie in a relatively short time. Pies with crusts on top had Mother's special designs. The chocolate, lemon and butterscotch pies usually had meringue on top, whereas the pumpkin pie had no topping on it. Pumpkin pie was frequently eaten with apple jelly generously spread on top. Our pies were usually cut into six pieces, and since the filling was quite thick, they made for hearty servings. We also had "snit" pie, made from pieces of apple dried in the sun and stored in a cloth bag until used. Various cobblers, such as cherry and apple, were looked forward to for dessert. These were usually served with cream or milk over them and sometimes we added sugar.

Two commonly made candies were chocolate fudge or taffy. Of course the chocolate fudge was quite thick and loaded with black walnut kernels. My mother usually made fudge alone, but the whole family got into the act on making taffy. Although my mother cooked the taffy, everybody helped pull it. Everyone was given a hunk of the taffy as it came off the stove, and was cooled enough to pull. Pulling consisted of stretching the taffy hunk to two or three feet, folding it over and pulling it again and again. The taffy changed texture as it was pulled. If it was made with white molasses, the taffy was white, but if it was made with black molasses, it turned beige or brown. The taffy was stretched into ropes about one-half to three-quarters of an inch thick, and cut in pieces about one inch long.

To pull the taffy, we smeared our hands with butter to keep the taffy from sticking to our fingers and hands. Butter had to be renewed several times during the pulling, as it was mixed into the taffy. The taffy was cut using my mother's scissors, which were also rubbed with butter to prevent sticking. Taffy was pulled in a cool place, so it was not a summertime project. The taffy set up and frequently got quite hard. The harder the taffy, the longer you had to keep it in your mouth before you could chew it.

Taffy was a somewhat dangerous candy, for it could pull any loose filling out of a tooth. Aunt Celia pulled an expensive dental bridge out one night at our home while eating taffy. Occasionally one of us boys would end up with non-white taffy. Mother said this was because our hands weren't spotless while pulling. That taffy was set aside for the puller to eat, so we each ate our own dirt. A common belief was that a boy would eat at least a peck of dirt during his childhood, and I am sure we met this standard.

Popcorn was always popular, and again was a wintertime treat. Prior to getting electricity we popped it over the fire in the kitchen cook stove. Two eyes of the cook stove and the intermediate eye support structure were removed, leaving an open area about eight inches by twenty inches over the wood coals to expose the popper. The popper was a screen box about 6" x 8" x 4" with a hinged top, which was mounted on a wooden handle about three feet long. The corn was put in the popper, the popper put over the opening of the stove, and the popper shaken so that all kernels would get hot to pop better. Letting the wooden handle slide on the stove top was easier than holding it up and allowed one to keep further from the stove.

The popped corn was dumped in a large pan and served to everyone who had a hand or pan to eat from. The popped corn was frequently salted and eaten dry. Sometimes sugar syrup was poured over it, which enhanced the flavor for those with a sweet tooth. Some of the popped corn with syrup was made into popcorn balls, which were frequently kept a day or so until we had eaten all of them. Popped corn was also threaded onto a string and this used as part of the Christmas decoration. Popping corn, like taffy pulling, was a social event. Later, we bought an electric popper and could then add butter while popping, which improved the taste considerably.

Ice cream was always a special treat. Various kinds were made such as vanilla, chocolate, peach, strawberry, banana and raspberry. Whole milk with generous portions of cream were used as the base ingredient, with the flavoring or fruit added. The fruit used was whatever was in season, and again generous quantities were added. Junkets were used to make the ice cream even smoother, giving it a rich texture. It was easier to make ice cream in the winter when there was ice available on the frozen ponds. In the warm weather we either got ice from Mr. Earl's ice house or bought it in town. Mother always made ice cream and cake for our birthdays and we invited our friends in to play and eat. There were no birthday gifts given except the gift of the cake and ice cream.

Our love of ice cream almost cost us our Mother one summer Sunday. Dad drove us into Mt. Jackson after church at Otterbein Chapel in our two-door Model A Ford to get ice for making ice cream. He put the ice at my mother's feet in the front and then made a sharp left turn. He had not latched her door and my mother fell out, but my father grabbed her by the legs before her head hit the pavement and there was no harm done. That was a close call!

Ice houses were built by the individual farmer and only about ten percent of the farms had one Several neighbors helped fill the ice house with ice from the ponds on the farm. The neighbors who helped were entitled to some of the ice as long as it lasted. The ice was not suitable for use in the home such as for ice tea and ice water, because the cows and horses drank out of the ponds and waded in them.

The inside of the ice house was about ten feet wide by fifteen feet long by twelve feet high, with part of the volume below grade. The walls were made of boards and were about twelve inches thick filled with sawdust. The sawdust was the insulation which kept the outside heat from melting the ice. The building frequently had an "A" roof and no door. An opening was provided near the top on one side or one end for access to put ice in and remove it. This cut down on the heat loss.

The bottom of the ice house had a thick layer of sawdust so that heat would not flow up from the earth, which was about sixty degrees F. Ice was put in the bottom of the ice house and then a thin layer of sawdust added. Then another layer of ice was added and then another layer of sawdust until the ice house was filled to within about three feet of the top. The remainder of the house was filled with sawdust to form a thick insulation layer on top. When ice was removed we were always careful to cover the remaining ice with a thick layer of sawdust to decrease the melting of the remaining ice. Ice was available until late in the summer, depending on the amount used and the quantity and quality of the insulating sawdust.

The meats we ate were mostly chicken and pork. Beef and fish were served much less frequently. The chickens we raised both for our food and for sale. We sold broilers that reached about two and a half pounds after fifteen weeks. We also sold eggs to the store and to the hatchery. We had fresh chicken at least on Sunday and then for school lunch a day or so following. Mother also made pressed chicken, which was sliced thick and made into sandwiches for school lunches.

Pork was a major meat that really provided quite a variety of meals. Various pork products such as ham, shoulder, side meat (bacon), sausage, liver, heart, brains, back bone, tenderloin, puddins and feet were served at various times. The hams and shoulders were usually sliced about one quarter inch thick and fried. The gravy was put over thick slices of homemade bread, and was it good! You could make a meal of just that, but we were required to eat our vegetables as well. Mother also made thick gravy and this was also frequently eaten over bread as well as over mashed potatoes. We didn't care much for the side meat, as the amount of lean was too small except for the year we had Berkshire hogs.

The liver, heart and brains were all fried. We considered the brains a delicacy, as there was such a small quantity per hog, for they are not big on brains. The backbone and ribs were usually cooked and served at supper. Stuffed sausage and puddins were fried. The loose puddins were simply heated before serving. We particularly liked our hotcakes with puddins and syrup for a special breakfast. Pigs' feet and ears were not very popular but, of course, we ate them with no complaining. Mother made souse out of what we did not eat, but we did not crave this any more than we did the feet and ears.

We ate mostly homemade bread, biscuits, rolls, corn bread and, rarely, store-bought bread. Mother baked bread once or twice a week, about six loaves at a time. Once in a while, we would run out of bread and Mother would send us to Painter's store for a loaf. My father would say, "Wind again" every time Mother bought store-bought bread. Several times a year Mother would have a special breakfast for us that consisted of toast and soft-boiled eggs. She would lay the homemade bread slices on the flattop surface of the stove to toast them, then quickly dip them in boiling water and serve them to us. We would break the soft-boiled eggs over the toast and just gorge ourselves over this special breakfast.

We grew a great variety of vegetables, as mentioned earlier. They were served fresh in season and canned or dried out of season. Mashed potatoes were a favorite as we enjoyed them with butter or gravy over them. Mashed potatoes were served the next night as fried potato cakes, which were about three inches in diameter and up to an inch thick and frequently mixed with chopped onions. These were also a favorite. We always had two or more vegetables at a meal and everyone ate a reasonable helping of each. The varieties of vegetables were potatoes, tomatoes, corn, beans, cucumbers, lettuce, cabbage, sweet potatoes, asparagus, salsify, parsnips, celery, rhubarb, turnips, etc. I liked raw turnips, and did not like cooked turnips, but I ate them just the same. Corn on the cob was always a favorite for family and guests.

We always ate at home, never in a restaurant. The only restaurant meal I ever ate growing up was at Hawkins Restaurant in Mt. Jackson. The policeman, Mr. Harry Ward, took Dick and me out to dinner the day we drove our cow, pulling the buggy, in the fire carnival parade. Restaurant eating was a luxury at that time, and we just never participated. Our money could be better spent on necessities. "Waste not, want not" was engraved into our minds.

We always had plenty of nourishing food, but the variety was limited, especially among the meats. There was never any complaining, such as "Do we have to have chicken again tonight?" The variety was in the vegetables and the dessert, but that might be the same for several meals in a row. We were required to eat a reasonable helping of everything served and then we could have seconds. We always considered ourselves fortunate to have plenty of good food and a warm home. There were people in the community less fortunate, and the more fortunate ones helped the less fortunate by gifts of food, clothing, and even firewood. The philosophy of "waste not, want not" applied to many other things than just food.

Our three meals were breakfast, dinner (noon) and supper, with supper being the only meal that we all ate together. Mother and Dad usually ate breakfast before we boys got up, for Dad left for work about six o'clock. We boys sorta ate at the same time, usually after we fed and watered the chickens. Our breakfast consisted of milk, eggs, cereal, pork and bread. We were not allowed to have coffee, a beverage likely to "stunt our growth." We frequently left the house eating an apple on our way to school.

Our school lunch usually consisted of two sandwiches, chicken or pork, cookies or cake, and an apple or pear. We carried our lunches in metal lunch boxes that could be used as a weapon in the event of a disagreement with a classmate. Damage to the lunch box would result in being disciplined when we got home.

Week days, supper was the heavy meal of the day, and we ate between six and eight o'clock. If Dad was going to be home before eight o'clock, we all ate together; otherwise Mother kept his supper hot for him. Supper was usually pork with vegetables and dessert. School homework was done before and after supper, depending on what time we ate, but homework was always completed before bedtime.

Sunday dinner was our big meal of the day on Sundays, and usually consisted of fried chicken, vegetables and desserts. The chickens were prepared on Saturday afternoon by catching the chicken, cutting off its head, holding it so that it would not flop around and bruise, scalding it, picking it, and singeing it to burn off any small hair. Mother would dress the chicken. Dessert was cake, pie, peaches, pears, or cookies.

## Chapter Seven

# WORK

As children, we did work for our immediate family and for the extended family. For Grandmother Bowman, we did essentially the same work as we did at home, but to a lesser degree. We would also spend a few days with Grandma Dellinger and Aunt Polly several times during the summer and help them in any way we could. We were rewarded by the pleasure of being with them and making life a little easier for them, and also by the fact that Grandma Dellinger would always give us some money. As we became older, we began doing the same work for other people as we did at home. As older kids, we were paid a fixed amount on a per day basis when we worked in the field for Grandma Bowman. Like my Grandmother Dellinger, she paid us proportionally when we did chores around the house, such as mowing the lawn and weeding the garden. We considered the money a bonus.

**The Garden**

The garden was the largest single work area at home. Work needed to be done commencing in early May and continued into the late fall and winter. The garden work described here sometimes was done only by us boys, and other times was done under the overall supervision of a parent.

We helped cut potatoes for planting, since planting was frequently done the same day the garden was plowed. Although we were usually at school while the garden was being plowed, disked, and harrowed, it would be ready for us to plant the potatoes when we came home from school. We helped drop the potato pieces in the row with the eyes up so that the potato sprout would break through the ground sooner. We frequently led the horse to cover the potatoes, for this was faster and left a smoother surface than if they were covered using a hoe.

As the spring continued, we helped in the planting of seeds and setting out of plants. We helped sow corn, string beans, butterbeans, peas, and cucumbers, and set out cabbage, tomatoes, sweet potatoes and celery plants.

During the spring and summer we sowed and set out other plants for cultivation and weeded them as needed. All plants were arranged so that they could be plowed in the beginning, but as certain plants such as tomatoes grew, some of them could not be plowed. We did not stake our tomatoes, for instance, so they would fall as the vines grew taller. The stalks were hoed between hills, and the weeds were killed in the process.

There were always weeds to be pulled, as well as cultivation and hoeing to be done. Weeds grew in many varieties, such as lamb's quarter, red roots, crab grass and foxtails. The weeds were always pulled right after a rain, if possible, because the ground was soft and pulling was easier. We had to dig the weeds out if it was dry, since they were stronger than we were. The weeds were kept out as much as practical so that they would not rob the vegetables of the plant food.

Cultivation was by a hand plow which had a large wheel up front, two handles, and a plow shovel behind the wheel. The plow was intended to be pushed by an adult, which was hard work. Since we were small and weak as compared to adults, we put a rope on the front of the plow, lowered the handles as far down as we could, and one of us pulled and the other pushed.

We had a cow we trained to pull the plow but the effort to get her enthusiasm up took more effort than we saved. This was definitely a novelty and not time or effort-effective. Sometimes my father would get a horse and plow everything that he could, but that, too, was far from perfect. Despite our leading the horse, it stepped on and ruined too many plants. Unlike a riding horse, a work horse has very big feet, sort of like the Clydesdales. Mules' feet are much smaller, and people who had mules often used them in the gardens.

At a young age, my brothers and I helped pick the vegetables as they matured and were ready for eating or preservation. Preservation was mostly by canning, but some vegetables such as beans and corn were sometimes dried. These were prepared for drying and placed on the back porch roof so that they would get the most sun. They were frequently covered with a window screen to keep the birds from enjoying the harvest. The peas and beans were picked, shelled and snapped as appropriate prior to canning. The shelling and snapping was frequently done after supper with the entire family helping.

Tomatoes and cucumbers were picked as they became ripe for canning and pickling. Mother did most of the canning preparation as well as the actual canning. Other vegetables, such as carrots, parsnips, etc., were harvested and preserved as necessary. The ears of corn were snapped off, shucked, silked and then the kernels cut off the cob for canning. Corn was somewhat difficult to can without spoiling, so our corn for canning was taken to a cannery operated by a husband-wife team. They also canned our peas. Celery was the last plant set out and as it grew, it was ridged up so that it would bleach white. The work associated with celery is described in the chapter on food.

Insect control was essential. This was done by applying poison and/or picking the bugs by hand. We would pick the potato bugs and bean beetles and put them in a can of kerosene to kill them. This was positive destruction of the bugs. It was not unusual to see a bug with white poison powder on it that had come over from a garden nearby. We dusted the plants using poison powder put in an old cloth sack with no hole in it.

We helped pick up potatoes as they were plowed out, using a horse and single shovel plow. The potatoes were then washed, graded, dried and taken to the cellar for storage. The cut potatoes were eaten first, so that they would not rot. We dug the sweet potatoes by hand, using a grubbing hoe to dig with. The sweet potatoes were preserved similarly to the Irish potatoes.

Our role in caring for the chickens included giving them scratch feed, morning and evening, and keeping mash in feeders for them at all times. Oyster shells and water were always kept in front of them. The water had to be thrown out at night during the winter in order to keep the water container from freezing. Warm water was given to them in the morning and during the day, Mother or Dad put out warm water as necessary to keep the water from freezing. The eggs were gathered at least twice a day to decrease breakage and also to keep from freezing during the winter. We boys gathered the eggs in the evening.

## Other Chores

The chicken roosts were cleaned by us boys about once a week. The manure was scraped off the roost into a wheelbarrow using a broad hoe. Each load was scattered over the pasture field or garden as fertilizer. This was carefully spread to ensure that all areas got covered and that none received too much because too much chicken manure could burn the grass.

About once a month the chicken house had to be cleaned, a task usually delegated to us boys. The process for this was to rake the loose litter off, sweep the floor, scrape any chicken manure off the floor and sweep it again. The chicken litter was sometimes spread on the field and other times dumped in the barnyard. This was a dusty, dirty job, but someone had to do it. Clean litter, consisting of straw or wood shavings, was then spread on the chicken house floor. The litter always worked to the back of the chicken house, as the chickens scratched on the floor. About once a week the loose litter was raked to the front and the chickens started the cycle all over. The chicken house had to be cleaned more often if the litter was not redistributed frequently.

Mother milked the cows every morning and evening, and our job was to care for the cows by cleaning the cow stable and bedding it with clean straw twice a day. This, of course, was unnecessary during the warmer weather when the cows stayed in the cow pasture. We would get the hay down from upstairs in the barn and put the hay in the hay racks for the cows, and would give the cows grain every morning and evening.

During the summer months we drove or rode the cows to my grandmother's for daytime pasture and brought them home in the evening for my mother to milk them. We kept the flies off the cow's front legs and belly, while one of us held the cow's tail so the cow would not beat my mother with it as she tried to switch the flies off her back.

The hogs required less care than the cows, but the hog pen had to be cleaned and bedded each day. We would also slop the hogs both morning and evenings. The slop consisted of water, food from the table, middlins and grains to supplement this. As we grew stronger, we held or helped hold the pigs to have my father put pig rings in their nose. This was to keep them from rooting up the ground. We also helped hold the pigs when Mr. Earl castrated them.

There were many miscellaneous chores we did or helped with around the home. We mowed the lawn using a push reel mower and as we got stronger we mowed between our fence and the road to improve appearances. We dug thistle and sand briers out of the pasture field and sometimes dug thistle out of adjoining fields. The neighbors' thistles were dug out to keep them from seeding into our field. It was our responsibility to keep the wood box on the back porch and the coal buckets in the living room full. We also helped clean house by dusting, shaking the rugs and scrubbing the floors, even though this was considered "girl work."

We took great delight in churning ice cream because this was not really work. Churning butter, on the other hand, was another job. Butter from our Jersey and Guernsey cows required only about one half hour to churn. I don't know what kind of cows my grandmother had, but Mother said they frequently churned almost all day! We usually spent one day picking blackberries and one day picking cherries each summer. One or both of our parents were always present because of the probability of accidents, such as rattlesnake bites or falling out of a tree. We were also much more productive when they were present, for some strange reason.

The majority of the work we did away from home was out in the fields on my Grandmother Bowman's farm. The first work I did there was at about the age of seven or eight, thinning corn by myself in the field below the barn. Where there were more than two corn stalks in a corn hill, I pulled the extras and packed dirt back around the roots. The corn was about six inches tall when I started and became too big for me to pull before I finished, so the men on the farm finished the job. I thinned about 25 rows each day, with the rows running toward the lower field from the house.

At Grandmother Bowman's farm, there was a slate spring beside the creek that provided cool clean water for drinking. I would go to the house at about mid-morning and mid afternoon for pie or cake to sustain me physically and mentally. It was a bit lonely out there all by myself in the hot sun. I remember getting very frustrated, but I would not give in and quit, probably largely due to the fact that I was being paid a quarter a day. The hired men were getting one dollar a day, so I was probably grossly overpaid considering the perks I was given. Later on we were given fifty cents and even later seventy-five cents a day for corn thinning.

Once Dick became old enough, we worked as a team, thinning corn for Uncle Clarence, Uncle John and Mr. Sam. We vowed we would not go back to Uncle Clarence's again until they got rid of the fleas his dogs had. We stayed with them for about a week and were pretty badly chewed up by the time we left, every bite looking like a hive.

We were given the light work to do, such as operating the buggy rake and hay tedder as well as loading hay. This consisted of driving the horse using check lines and operating the various levers to dump the hay and kick the hay over. The men pitched the hay up onto the wagon and we placed it and packed it down. If the hay was pitched up correctly, about all we had to do was stamp it down. We also helped to pile the hay in "easy to pitch" piles prior to loading the hay wagons. We drove the horse to pull the hay fork, which carried the hay up into the mow when we were small.

We worked in the mow as we got older. Working in the mow consisted of moving the hay from the center of the mow to both sides for even distribution. This was always a hot and frequently dusty operation, with clover dust being the worst.

Us boys also helped cultivate the corn using a double- or triple-shovel plow pulled by one horse. This consisted of driving the horse using a single lead line and operating the plow at the proper place and depth. The corn for the silo was cut green and stacked in small bundles for easy loading on the ensilage wagons. We never worked in the silo during silo filling, but we frequently threw ensilage down from the silo in the winter to feed the cattle. The other corn was not cut until after we started to school so Saturday was the only day we could help cut and shock corn.

A saddle was made of four hills of corn by tying the tops of the stalks together. The corn stalks were cut and the corn placed around the saddle with the tassels up. One method was called hugging, in which you cradled the stalks in one arm and cut them off at the ground with a corn chopper in the other hand. The bundle was carried to and placed against the saddle. The other method was to chop the corn down, place it in piles and then pick up the piles and place them against the saddle. The final product was a corn shock which included the corn stalks from a given number of corn hills such as sixteen by sixteen square. The shock was complete when the stalks were tied using binder twine near the top.

The corn was shucked out as time permitted, and again, we could only help on Saturdays, so our effort could not have been considered significant.

Another job that boys could do was take the horses to the blacksmith to be shod. The blacksmith shop was fascinating with a forge to heat the steel red hot to easily form it to fit the horse's hooves. The hand-operated drill presses were also interesting since all that we had at home was a brace with wood bits and a few steel cutting bits. Dad also put rubber tires on his tractor at the blacksmith shop. This consisted of taking solid truck tires, sometimes ten inches wide and three inches thick, sawing the rubber and steel and then bending them to a large radius to fit the wheels. I never saw them do this, so I don't know how they did it with the little machinery they had.

We helped shock wheat on harvest days and loaded the sheaves on the wagons on thresh days. The men pitched the sheaves up onto the wagons. One summer we helped a little, and watched the crushing of rocks for the half-mile of road into the farm. These limestone rocks had been blasted out of the field and were stacked along the road. An old single-cylinder horizontal gasoline engine drove the rock crusher. It had an open water cooler on the top of the engine. The oiling system was the drip method and this was hand set for each oiling cup.

We were fascinated to find that the workers cooked field corn in the shuck using this water cooler by putting the ears into its near-boiling water. They left the shucks on because the water was oily, but when the shucks were removed, the corn was clean and good. We helped them eat the corn. However, the corn became too hard in a few days, so the novelty disappeared quickly.

Salem Church abutted our land, and it was our job to keep the inside and outside of Salem Church clean and the grass mowed. We would also mow the cemetery lots where both sides of our family were buried. The church members got together about once each summer and cleaned the entire cemetery. This was all done by hand, as there were no power mowers available. Mowing scythes were one of the most useful tools as the grass, weeds, vines, etc. were quite tall.

Uncle Fred owned the "Gochenour Farm" near Woodstock and we worked for him on this farm, doing things like corn thinning, harvesting and haymaking. Our first cousin, Chalmers, also worked for Uncle Fred, and we all traveled with an adult to the farm. Mr. Jim Bauserman drove us in Uncle Fred's 1935 Plymouth and his driving habits were both humorous and dangerous. He would stop *after* he passed a stop sign, usually in the middle of the road he was entering, and he would blow the car horn when he approached a railroad crossing. It was understandable that we had some safety concerns.

We discussed this driving at the supper table several evenings until one evening mother said "I do not want to have Mr. Jim for supper again tonight" which ended the supper review of the day's drive. Chalmers was always so much fun to be with and the day's work was just one big laugh, but we were also very productive. One day at a work break for water Chalmers had the thermos jug under his arm and was laughing so hard the jug fell and broke. We each put up equal money to buy Aunt Mae a new jug, but she would not accept the money. We always enjoyed working for Uncle Fred and Aunt Mae.

Uncle Fred always called each of us "Buck" for some reason. It was always "Buck, you do this" or "Buck, you do that," but always "Buck." Uncle Fred was big on keeping weeds to a very minimum. He referred to the weeds as "thilth," so he would say "Buck, pull all the thilth out of the hay field and bring it to the washhouse to burn." This killed the seeds. The thilth included Nardock, wild carrots, milkweed, thistles, etc., all of which were very prolific. Each stalk seemed to have hundreds of seeds, which could take over a field if the weeds were left to reseed. Uncle Fred later burned down the washhouse when the burning weeds got out of control.

Another job we helped do was driving the cattle to pasture in the spring and back to my grandmother's in the fall. The longest drive ever made by Dad, Dick and me was to Pugh's Run. I remember that well for we stopped the drive about noon at a country store. Dad bought us potted meat and crackers, which was such a delight compared to ham, tenderloin, chicken, etc. at home! After lunch, we continued the drive to the pasture fields. Dick and I would walk in front and block the lanes to people's houses to keep the cattle from going there. Then we would sneak past the cows so that we could repeat the same operation at the next lane or opening off the road.

Overall, work was pleasant and we had fun doing it. This is where we got started telling jokes, some of which I still remember. Single individual jobs sometimes left a lot to be desired, such as getting "thilth" out of the hay, wheat and corn fields. Everyone worked well together with no one loafing, and all in a good mood, which contributed to the comradeship we enjoyed.

Almost everyone in the community worked for themselves, someone else, or in the home. There was one notable exception, Joe Lutz. He is reported to have said, "I will work until I am twenty-one but never again after twenty-one." To the best of my knowledge he never broke his word. He just bummed around the community, and I never knew how he was able to manage financially. My father stated that when he drove from Harrisonburg to Mt. Jackson, which was twenty-five miles, if Joe was the last person he saw in Harrisonburg, he was frequently the first person he saw when he arrived in Mt. Jackson! Some people just have a knack for getting around.

**Figure 10**
Grandmother Dellinger Splitting Wood

**Figure 11**
Joseph Earl Bowman & His Hart Parr Tractor

## Chapter Eight

## PLAY—ONE BOY, TWO BOYS, THREE BOYS

We played at every opportunity--at home, games at school, and while hunting, trapping, and fishing. We went skating, went on picnics, were interested in girls, etc., many examples of which are described in other sections. Our play at school is described under the section "School." We played at home with relatives and friends who lived nearby. Dick and I played together and worked together much more than Alden and I did, since Alden was older and spent a great deal of his free time working at Grandma Bowman's farm. There was only so much farm work appropriate for young boys, so Dick and I worked more at home, and consequently played there more.

As is often the case with young boys, we tried to mimic our father's work in our play. He spent most of his time with machinery, so Dick and I did the same, but to a lesser degree. We had no machines to play with except our "express" wagon, which we used almost all the time in one way or another.

All of the old discarded farm machinery was put on a large limestone rock in the Painter field, which was aptly known by all of us as "The Rock." Machinery included items such as corn plows, wagons, buggies, plows, threshing machines and even our family Model T Ford. This old machinery was the source of most of the parts we assembled into our "machine." Anything on The Rock was considered fair game for us and much of it was impossible for us to dismantle. We had few tools to work with, the main ones being a few old wrenches, a buggy wrench, a hammer, and a bullet mold which we used for pliers. Unfortunately this bullet mold was lost somewhere during the years and is lost forever.

A play day would consist of pulling our wagon and tools to The Rock, which was about three quarters of a mile from home, taking off what we could and hauling it home. The odds of getting anything significant off this old machinery were low for several reasons. We were young and small, not sure of how things were put together, had few tools, and much of the machinery was quite rusty-- four good reasons for low productivity. But we enjoyed it. We took the shafts, cog wheels, pulley, chains, etc. and rigged them so that everything turned and made noises, and we called this our threshing machine, which we cranked. The only output from this threshing machine as we turned the shaft, pulley, and chains was noise in which we reveled.

We played town ball in our pasture field but seldom had enough boys for a full game. We played football usually with less then ten boys. During a full moon we frequently played football at night, but this had to be planned in advance because the pasture field had to be cleaned up before the game. You could dodge the obstacles during the day but they were deadly at night. Another less vigorous game was croquet, which was usually played in the yard. We cleared a croquet field in the pasture field but the cows would walk through the wire fence and mess up the area. We quickly gave up on that endeavor.

Aunt Mae frequently played Rook, Old Maid and Pig with us even though cards were slightly frowned on due to the stigma of gambling. Of course we played cowboys and Indians with various guns. Some of the guns we made out of wood and/or metal, some were store bought and one was real. The real one was a "Horse Pistol" which my Grandmother Bowman gave me. It was a cap and ball therefore it was safe, for it was unloaded and had been for years. The story goes that Great Grandpa Ephriam Bowman used this pistol to try to prevent John Kline from marrying his daughter Jinny. He failed to stop them and Jinny rode behind John on the horse in their daring escape. They married. The revolver was a six shot and about the size of an Army forty-five.

This cowboys and Indian play would frequently end up in the churchyard at Salem Lutheran Church. There were very slender pine trees about thirty feet tall in the back churchyard. We would climb as near to the top as we dared and would swing back and forth for the thrill. Swinging back and forth near the top would then degenerate into a more daring game whereby each person would sway his tree near someone else's and try to knock him out of his tree. Miraculously, no one ever got hurt in this game, if that is what you would call it.

There were no riding horses left on the farm because the automobile had taken over as the predominant form of transportation and riding horses had become a luxury. We would ride the work horses on Sunday, but only for a short time and only at a walk, since Sunday was a day of rest for the horses as well as for people. Another reason for not running the horses was that sometimes they would hit their feet together and tear off or loosen the horseshoes.

We engaged in another form of play that no one else in the area ever did to the best of our knowledge. Mother and Dad kept a Heifer calf to grow into a cow to replace a cow that was growing old and decreasing in milk production. The calf, which we named "Judy," was trained to pull our "Express Wagon." We replaced the wagon tongue with a pair of home made shaves, made a collar for the calf from a gas tank hose wrapped with burlap bags, and used rope for traces. The calf was difficult to train, probably because this performance was not in her genes. She would lie down and break the shaves, but we did not give up. She was led wearing a halter.

As our calf grew larger and older she graduated to bigger and better things. We fitted her with a riding bridle with a bit in her mouth and drove her with check lines. Before she was a year old we were driving her in a "Stud Horse Cart" (which Mr. Sam Hollar gave us) with two people on the cart and frequently one small person riding on the Heifer. We used her a few times to pull the garden plow but without too much success. The highlight of the entire saga was when we entered her in the Mt. Jackson fire carnival parade. She pulled a one-horse buggy with Dick and me in the buggy driving her with check lines. Dad had Sam Myers walk alongside to help if she got out of control or could not pull us up the hills. She behaved magnificently. She soon became fresh (had a calf) which ended her career in the limelight.

There were many Sam Hollar stories. "Mr. Sam," as we called him, spent many hours building a wooden gate to close the lane coming to his farm so that his stock would not leave. He installed the gate on Saturday and went to town that night, as was sorta the custom. When he came home late that night he forgot about the gate and drove right through the closed gate! Of course much of the community heard about his encounter with the gate and everyone came to their own conclusion as to why the accident happened.

Another time Mr. Sam got up at night, loaded the shotgun and started to leave the bedroom. Mrs. Margaret said, "Sam, what are you doing?" He said, "Shh—sh." She assumed he had heard something or someone at the chicken house. Chickens were vulnerable to animals and also subject to being stolen by people. He was barefooted and in his night shirt. He went to the chicken house, fired the shotgun and woke up. He said it must have taken him thirty minutes to walk back to the house over the gravel and briars. Many people walked in their sleep. My father walked in his sleep but apparently was cured when he walked out of the house on a cold winter night and caught cold.

Swimming was essentially nonexistent; however, we did play in the Hamburg Run and creek at Grandma Dellinger's. There was one spot in the Hamburg Run on Mr. Earl's farm that was about two feet deep. Many of the boys learned to swim at this spot, but I was unable to get the hang of it. The creek at my grandmother's was too small and shallow to swim in, but we did catch a few fish there. We built sod dams with stakes, but they leaked too much or the dams washed away, so we spent hours demonstrating that we were not dam builders. On hot summer days we enjoyed playing in the water under the large willow trees.

We would go frog hunting several times each summer and frequently did quite well. This is described under "Food." On one of the frog nights we were on Mr. Pence's property at Hamburg Run working our way upstream. As we approached a road that crossed the run, a young dating couple stopped on the bridge and the lady yelled and said, "Are you getting any?" My reply was "Yes, are you?" And there the conversation ended and they drove off. We'll never know the answer. Catching pigeons was another pastime, which was more play than work. It, too, is covered in the "Food" section. We caught them for food and to sell but the real reason was that it was a challenge and none of us would have done it except for wanting to be macho.

Bicycling was a rare pleasure for us because we owned no bicycles. There was never anything that we wished for more than having a bicycle. "If wishes were horses beggars would ride" was a favorite comment when the wishes got out of hand. This was one of the times that we understood that there was a difference between "want" and "need" and also a difference in being able to "pay for something" and being able "to afford something." J.R. and Randolph Foltz, schoolmates, had bicycles. When we played together we rode their bicycles. They were completely unselfish with regard to letting us ride their bicycles.

Ice-skating was one of our favorite winter fun activities. We usually skated at Mr. Green Clanahan's pond about one quarter mile from home. The ice was safe when it was at least two inches thick. The pond was about two hundred feet across and the ice would visibly bend as someone skated across it. We broke through occasionally, which reminded us of the third grade reader story of the red rooster. The rooster was told the berries were not ripe, but he said, "I can't wait" and got very sick from eating the berries. He was told that the ice was too thin, but he said, "I can't wait," went out on the ice, broke through and drowned. No one drowned, but walking home with wet clothes at below freezing temperature was the least enjoyable part of the ice skating experience.

On freezing evenings we would frequently gather at the pond for night skating. We would build a fire using kindling wood and old tires to keep warm when not skating. We built the fire in the middle of the pond and once it melted through the ice, the fire would go out and it was time to call it a night.

Sledding was another winter sport that we spent many hours enjoying. For years, the ten families on the hill would frequently get together and go sliding. Our parents and many of the children used a coasting board. The coasting board was about twenty-five feet long and about fifteen inches wide. It was quite flexible, being only about one inch thick and was curved up at the front end. One sat on the board with his arms and legs around the person in front of him. About twenty people could get on a twenty-five-foot board.

There was a rope fastened to the front and tied at both corners. The first person steered or attempted to steer the board using the ropes in the same manner as check lines. After everyone was in place on the board at the top of the hill, the last person would push the board to get it started and then jump on. Once in a while, depending on the person steering and how the passenger leaned, the board would turn over and dump everyone off. I do not remember any serious injuries.

Some boys had sleds, whereas we did not. We made several sleds; some with wooden runners and some with steel buggy tires on the runner, but none were very successful. We rode sleds as singles or doubles. Sleds would go faster than a coasting board, but coasting boards had the right of way. Furthermore, when our parents were on the coasting board, they definitely had the right of way. Our coasting and sledding was usually done on the crust that formed after the snow had partially melted.

Running into a wire fence, especially in the dark, was a hazard that usually caused cuts and scratches. The worst I was ever hurt while sledding occurred across from Joe Myers's home. The crust was just thick enough to hold up the sled but not thick enough to walk on. Alden had walked up the hill and left holes in the snow. I was lying on the sled, which was normal, and Dick was lying on top of me (we only had two sleds for three boys). As we went barreling down the hill I cut across the tracks Alden had made. The sled broke through the crust and we both slid over the front of the sled. Dick's weight pushed my face into the crust, leaving me with hardly a single spot on my face that was not scratched and bleeding. That ended sledding for that day.

Picnics, fire carnivals and lawn parties are included under socializing. We always tried to pair up with a girl to make the evening more enjoyable.

Our sports program in high school was limited to play time before school and at noon hour. I was not allowed to play on the football team because of the severe scarlet fever that I had in my sophomore year.

My last fight in school occurred while playing football before school. One of the other team players was, in my opinion, being too rough on some of our team's smaller members, so I championed their cause. Our principal was very tough on discipline and an excellent teacher. When I got to his class near noon, my right eye was getting pretty black. Mr. Swartz said "Elmore, what happened to your eye?" I was not about to give him the story, so I said "Something hit me in the eye." If he had quizzed me further I would have had to tell him it was a fist, but he spared me this.

When we were small we had a few toys, all of which were still serviceable when we quit playing with them. We spent many hours making toys for our pleasure. One of these was a log wagon pulled by two horses. About the only tools we had were pocketknife, wood chisel, compass saw, coping saw, handplane, and the horse head, described elsewhere. This toy was still in the attic long after I had left home. Rope swings in our trees were not practical, for the trees were planted the same year I was born, so I was always too large for the trees during those early years.

Radio was another entertainment. Alden won a Crosley table radio at the Edinburg fire carnival in 1932. It was an AC superhetrodyne with a 175-kilocycle intermediate frequency strip. We did not get electricity until 1934, so we had no radio until then. Some people had battery radios but we did not. Dad took our radio down to Mr. Raymond's, who had electricity, and they listened to the election results of Hoover and Roosevelt. We had our regular weekday programs that we listened to; however, taking care of the chickens, cows, hogs, garden and firewood chores came first. It's amazing how quickly a couple of boys can get a lot done with the right incentive.

The programs I remember were Jack Armstrong the All American Boy (Wheaties), Little Orphan Annie (Ovaltine), Tom Mix (Ralston) and Terry and the Pirates. These were each fifteen-minute programs, including commercials, to sell the products sponsoring them as well as gifts to promote the sales. You were required to send a box top and ten cents to receive gifts such as rings, pictures, whistles and small noise makers. The manufacturers were appealing to the children—some things never seem to change. Later in the evening the family all listened to Amos and Andy, Lum and Abner from Pine Ridge Arkansas and Uncle Ezra from his powerful little five-watter down in Rosedale, Tennessee. Lowell Thomas was the newscaster we listened to for the world news.

Special play activities were associated with each holiday. Cracking Easter eggs was always quite a contest, especially at school. Almost everyone brought hard-boiled Easter eggs as part of lunch. The contest was to see whose egg would be the last to break. One person would hold his or her egg and the second person would strike the egg with his or her egg. The one that did not break would then go through the same ritual until there was only one unbroken egg, which was the winner. The small end of the egg is the strongest with the long sides the most fragile, so you held your egg so that the aggressor could only hit the small end. Sometimes someone would use a wooden egg, but if that was found out a fight was frequently the end result. We always tried to get a few guinea eggs for Easter as these were the most difficult to break. A guinea egg always won.

One summer I spent a week with Uncle Claude, Aunt Celia, Claude, Jr. and Maggie at their home in Washington, D.C. The whole family took turns taking me to see different points of interest. Everything I saw was not only interesting but also new because I had never been to the city more than once before. I rode to Washington with them in their 1935 Ford, and Claude, Jr. had an ivory skull head as the gear shift knob. Aunt Celia was not amused when it came off in her hand as she shifted gears!

The week of visiting Washington, D.C. had a "once in a lifetime" event, a parade honoring "Wrong Way Corrigan" who supposedly had flown to Europe by mistake. The public buildings, White House, Congress, Jefferson Memorial, Lincoln Memorial, Washington Monument, zoo and Smithsonian Institute were some of the many areas we toured.

Aunt Mae took me to New York City in 1942 for a week's visit with Uncle Harry and Aunt Katherine. We saw the sights of New York City including Grant's Tomb, Staten Island, Brooklyn Bridge, Barnum and Bailey Circus, Broadway plays, and many other points of interest. Aunt Mae and I traveled by ourselves during the day while Uncle Harry and Aunt Katherine worked. It was a delightful visit.

As children, we were left on our own to entertain ourselves; however, Mother was nearby and I am sure she monitored us. One day Dick and I were playing with the hand pushed reel mower, which was sort of a no-no. Dick got his hand cut when it got between the knife and reel. We told my mother that he cut it on a broken glass bottle and we produced the broken bottle as evidence that we were unfortunate, not careless or dumb.

We always had several pet cats, which we played with for amusement. Every now and then in the hot summer we would take the cats to Uncle John's pond, which was only thirty feet in diameter. We would throw a cat to the center of the pond and when it swam to shore, catch it again and throw it back in the middle. We probably had some tired cats, but there was no sign of any harm done.

We played along my grandmother's creek during the hot summers. We tried to catch fish or frogs even though we always threw them back since they were too small to eat. We would reach into holes in the creek bank and frequently come out with a nice frog. One day I reached into a hole and pulled out a snake instead of a frog. That was the last time we ever reached into creek bank holes.

Further demonstrating that even seemingly tame animals deserve a healthy respect, one day we were playing ball in our field and Hazel and Frances rode by on two of Uncle John's mules. Hazel was on the mule named Jack. I yelled, "Get up Jack!" and he bucked Hazel off onto the road, causing her to cut her forehead. Apparently, she never told on me, because I heard nothing about the incident from my parents. I learned a lesson that day!

Our parents left us to entertain ourselves because they did not have time to play with us during the day. We frequently tried to build a boat to use in the pond. We would use whatever scrap lumber we could find and nail the boards together as tight as we could. Large cracks remained, too large to swell up in the water. We would scrape tar off the road where it puddled during the day, and use it to fill in the cracks between the boards. Something was wrong with our technique. Somehow, we never built a boat but always unintentionally built a submarine.

My grandfather's old cornshucker was stored in a shed at Salem Church, and we plundered it for parts just as we did the machinery on "The Rock." We even used the side boards of the shed to build our boats. The cornshucker supported the building, or the building would have fallen down.

We played horseshoes using the old worn out and broken shoes from my grandmother's farm horses. Some of the shoes were large, some medium and some small but we used all of them. We even used some old mule shoes that we found. These were somewhat the shape of the letter omega in the Greek alphabet. Some other tools and products we made for play and work were benches, tool handles, corn thinners and corn choppers. We also had a little play-work business of making yard ornaments for sale. These cut-out ornaments were of boys, girls, animals and birds painted in bright colors. We put pins in the bottom of them so that they could be stuck in the lawn. This was a "self-supporting" hobby.

Some of the things we had fun doing were exercises such as chinning, skin-the-cat and push-ups. We always tried to beat the competition. Technique was important; for example, the way you held your hands in chinning could make a great deal of difference. Skinning-the-cat consisted of jumping up and grasping a tree limb with both hands, next pulling up and thrusting your body between your arms and letting your legs dangle; then reverse the motion and go back to the starting position. Repeat the cycle. The person with the greatest number of cycles was the winner.

I do not know how old I was, but my first movie was "Trail of the Lonesome Pine" at the Edinburg Theater. It only cost ten cents but we did not have many ten cents to spend on the movies. Will Rogers and Joe E. Brown were favorites during their time and there was a serial on Saturday night.

I do not remember anyone in the neighborhood or school shooting marbles, even though we had marbles (but maybe not ALL of them). I guess we just did not know how to shoot them. Steelies would have been easy to come by due to the failed ball bearing in the various farm machines. Other games that we played were checkers, chinese checkers, carom, dominoes and a toy version of pinball.

When I was growing up, we were required to create most of our own fun which, in turn, caused us to be innovative. I have always felt that this was good training and preparation for life.

**Figure 12**
Dick & Twyman Elmore With Cow-In-Training

**Figure 13**
Twyman Elmore Bowman Riding Trained Cow

Chapter Nine

# HUNTING AND TRAPPING

No one would ever accuse the Bowman boys of being avid hunters. Although we were not big on either hunting or trapping, we did both to some degree, for both recreation and income purposes. We hunted rabbits, squirrels, pigeons, frogs, turtles, skunks, possum and crows. We trapped rabbits, skunks, opossums, and sometimes a housecat by mistake. Our hunting and trapping was all done within a mile and a half of our home, so all travel was by the "pick-them-up and put-them-down" method.

We trapped for muskrats one winter only and never caught one. They were just too smart for us, but other boys trapped them quite successfully and sold the pelts for fifty cents to two dollars. Trapping rabbits was another unsuccessful venture for us. However, trapping skunks was a different story; we were somewhat successful, sometimes catching 15 or 20 a year. We trapped skunks using single or double-spring steel traps set in their runs. A "run" was where the skunks traveled, and not being too smart, they did not sense the traps as a muskrat or fox would have done. We killed skunks with a club or shot them with a rifle while still in the trap. Two mandatory maneuvers were necessary: stay upwind, and face the skunk eyeball to eyeball. If one failed to strictly follow both of these admonitions, he might find himself shunned, especially indoors when it was warm.

We would check the traps before we went to bed and empty any traps that had game in them. Checking our traps one Sunday night at my grandmother's, we discovered that we had a skunk. I had a new hat, so I gave it to Dick to wear so that I would have no chance of getting skunk smell on it when I killed the skunk. All went as planned; however, Dick was downwind, and my new hat was some kind of stinking for a few days. Clothes that became stinky were hung outdoors for several days to dissipate the odor. Increased heat or moisture would increase the odor. Buyers who made a living in the winter buying and selling pelts picked up the pelts at our house.

Night hunting for skunks and opossums was also popular. We were not permitted to take any guns because guns our parents considered guns too dangerous for night hunting. There were usually three or four of us hunting together, and each person had a flashlight. We would walk through pasture fields, cornfields, woods, etc., spread apart to cover more area. Each person had a heavy cane that was used to kill the targeted animals. Usually we had a dog or two, and although they were pets rather than real hunting dogs, sometimes they would tree a skunk or an opossum. If the opossum was up a tree, we would throw rocks at it and try to knock it out of the tree. If that failed, one person would climb the tree and shake the limb until it fell to the ground. The favorite place to find an opossum was in a persimmon tree. We also liked persimmons, so when we got to a persimmon tree it was automatically time for a hunt break.

Skunks and opossums would be skinned and their hides put on stretcher boards for drying. It was very important when skinning the skunk not to puncture its defense system because one could again quickly become quite unpopular. If the weather got warm the pelts might spoil and have to be thrown away. Possum pelts sold for 25 to

50 cents each, and the skunk pelts sold for 50 cents to $2.00 per pelt. Skunks were graded number one, two, three or four with one being the best rating. A number one had either no white at all or just a very small white spot on its head. A number two had more white and a number three had white stripes halfway down its back. The number four had white stripes, sometimes running the full length of the body.

Several times each summer we would go frog gigging along the nearby creeks and ponds and around Hamburg Run. The ideal frog gigging party consisted of four people, two on each side of the small creek. We would use flashlights to find the frogs and either catch the frogs by hand or spear them with the gigs. We would cross-search the other bank and shine the light on the frog to be caught. Our gigs were homemade from the four-tooth section of an old garden rake. These did not tear up the frogs like the ones made for true gigging purposes. One had to hold the frog down with his gig, reach down and get the frog by hand because the gig's tines had very small burrs on them.

We usually caught many large frogs, and Mother would dress and cook them for us. We ate the front legs, the back, and the hind legs. Mother would usually fry them for breakfast after soaking them in saltwater overnight. The saltwater soak kept the frogs from twitching while they were frying. This is discussed in more detail under "Food."

The frogs were put in a burlap bag for easy carrying. We dressed the frogs, keeping the hind legs, front legs and backs of the large frogs and only the hind legs of the smaller frogs. Mother would fry them for breakfast or supper, whenever all the family could be there. I recall thinking that the taste of fried frog's legs is similar to that of a small fried chicken.

We would occasionally catch a mud turtle while frog hunting and bring it home. We would put it in a barrel of water and feed it cornmeal for a couple of weeks. We would then dress the turtle and fry the meat similar to chicken. There are supposed to be seven kinds of meat in a turtle. As an example, the neck tastes like frog, which is one of the tastiest of the meats.

The amount of meat that could be harvested from squirrels and rabbits in return for the effort of hunting them rendered those animals of minimal value, but we thoroughly enjoyed hunting and eating the meat. We hunted rabbits using an old single-shot 22-caliber rifle that had belonged to my grandfather. The bore was enlarged because my grandfather used shot shells in it for birds when he was recovering from an illness. Birds were easier to hit using shot shells because they had about 100 small pellets which spread out over a large area, as compared to a single "22" slug. The bolt mechanism would not eject the shell casing after firing, so we used a stiff wire as a ramrod to knock them out.

We could not seem to shoot the rabbit unless we spotted it sitting still. We could barely hit him stationary, much less when running. Mr. Clayton would not buy any rabbits unless they were trapped in a box trap. We had our box traps set most of the winter, but I cannot remember ever catching a rabbit. Instead, once in a while, we would inadvertently catch a house cat, but house cats could not be sold, whereas a trapped rabbit would sell for 10 cents. We all tracked rabbits in the snow, but never caught one, since evidently they were faster than we were.

In about 1938, isolated cases of tularemia, known to us as "rabbit fever," began to show up in our area. Grandma Dellinger and Aunt Polly died from rabbit fever, which ended our interest in rabbits. Their sickness with rabbit fever followed this sequence of events: My uncle shot a rabbit near my Grandma's house, brought it to the house, then skinned and dressed it. Aunt Polly handled the rabbit when she cut it up for cooking and put it into water to soak. It was very unusual for Grandma to enter directly in food preparation because that was Aunt Polly's forte, but in this case, Grandma changed the water during soaking.

My uncle did not get rabbit fever, but Grandma and Aunt Polly did. The reason given was that he had no scratches or open wounds on his hands for the bacteria to enter his body, but Aunt Polly and Grandma did. Grandma died within two months and Aunt Polly within four months. Mr. Painter, who lived near us, also got rabbit fever. He recovered, but was left with physical weakness. No one ever dressed a rabbit that appeared to be the least bit sick, but that was apparently no assurance that the disease would be avoided. Vulnerability to the disease occurred during exposure to it before cooking. Eating a cooked rabbit that had rabbit fever caused no ill effects.

We were also less than successful in our hunting squirrels. The only one I remember getting was one that was driven out of the woods during hunting season and ended up in Mrs. Lena's plum tree. I shot it, and mother made squirrel soup for Dick while he was recovering from having his tonsils removed. Crows were considered a nuisance, so we tried to kill them. But here again they were smarter than we were, and every time we shot, feathers flew along with the crow.

We had more success hunting pigeons. We hunted pigeons at night in barns, sheds and silos. We would use a flashlight to blind the pigeon and then would climb up and catch the pigeon by hand. I do not know why we did not fall and hurt ourselves badly, but I can't remember anyone ever getting hurt catching pigeons. We ate the pigeons or sold them alive to Mr. Clayton. Pigeons were picked dry, unlike chickens, which were scalded before being picked. A pigeon sold for about ten cents.

Chapter Ten

# CHURCH

Shenandoah County was predominantly Protestant and the Hamburg community was completely Protestant. Hamburg had Lutheran and Reform Churches only. Nearby communities had Dunkard, United Brethren, Baptist and some other churches in addition to the Lutheran and Reform churches. My father and his family were Lutherans and attended the Zion Lutheran church at Headquarters community. My mother and her family were United Brethren and attended the United Brethren church at Conicville. Alden joined the Lutheran church and Dick and I joined the United Brethren church.

The Lutheran church had four churches in the charge with the parsonage located at Zion Church. The four churches were Zion, Conicville, Fort Valley and Hamburg. The church at Hamburg joined our home property and was called Salem Lutheran Church. The minister would preach at each church every second week, sometimes before Sunday school and sometimes after Sunday school. Salem's congregation dwindled as families changed, and Sunday school was discontinued when I was about four or five years old.

We took care of the Salem Lutheran Church, which entailed cleaning, mowing, building fires in the winter, etc. The two trees in front of the church had large roots above the ground so mowing was difficult. In addition, the trees had a terrific underground root system and the roots sprouted up through the ground wherever they went. The roots went from the front of the church to forty feet behind the church and also under the road in front of the church. Sprouts grew in my uncle's pasture field across the road as well as forty feet behind the church. The sprouts provided my parents with an inexhaustible supply of switches. Some years later my uncle poisoned the fence row across the road from the church, which killed the two big trees. If this had happened 20 years earlier my parents would have had to find another source of "persuaders."

Salem Church closed in the mid-forties, even though the church attendees averaged three hundred percent of the number of members. There were only five members. My father bought the church for $1540.00 in 1947. This gave him an additional half-acre of land and kept someone from setting up housekeeping adjacent to our property. The wrong family, with sticky fingers, could have played havoc with our flock of chickens.

We attended Sunday school and service at the Zion Lutheran Church for many, many years. Mother taught the young people's class at Zion even though she belonged to the United Brethren church. The young people all wanted her for the teacher since she made the material very interesting. Her experience as a schoolteacher was a considerable aid to her in this work. Mother and Dad were active in the church not only teaching but also singing and participating in Christmas programs, church picnics, and the like.

The United Brethren Church consisted of six churches in the charge: Edinburg, Conicville, Hawkinstown, Mount Hermon, Otterbein Chapel and Columbia Furnace. The parsonage was located at Edinburg. We attended church at Conicville, which was the smallest, and there was never any Sunday school during my time in the church. Service was held once a month at two o'clock p.m. and Mother played the organ. The roof was blown off during a severe windstorm and the church closed. The church building was torn down and the land divided between the two adjacent homeowners.

After the Conicville United Brethren Church closed, Mother, Dick and I moved our membership to the Otterbein Chapel, where we are still members.

The church yard at Otterbein Chapel was a favorite "parking" spot for young people to gather in the evening.

**Figure 14**
Otterbein Chapel United Methodist Church

Chapter Eleven

# SCHOOL

Two schools, the Hamburg three-room grade school and Triplett High School, shaped our formative years prior to going out into the work force or attending college.

**Hamburg Grade School**

The Hamburg grade school, built in 1910 near Eckard's store, was a three-classroom school with all three classrooms located on the first floor. The total enrollment was a nominal 80 to 90 students with three teachers, one designated as principal. The second floor of the frame school house consisted of a large kitchen and an auditorium. The kitchen contained a wood stove, some tables and sort of a counter. The kitchen was used at night school functions to serve refreshments, such as cake, ice cream and hot dogs. These were contributed by the parents, sold by the League and the money used by the school for items not provided by the county. These items were costume material and other things that the teachers needed as teaching aids. The teachers also spent some of their own money on teaching aids.

The auditorium was used for assemblies, which were held on certain mornings of the week. The school teachers directed several programs during the year which were given at night and were well attended. Occasions such as Halloween, Christmas, Easter and the end of the school year were program times. The programs consisted of recitation, skits, singing groups, and the like so that everyone could participate.

Spelling bees were also held in the auditorium about once a year. Two knowledgeable parents were selected as the team leaders, and they chose up sides, picking the best spellers first on down to the less-accomplished spellers. This did not cause any problems. Mr. Kagey and my mother were usually the first two picks. The two teams lined up down the sides of the auditorium facing each other. The moderator gave a word to spell to one side and then the other, starting with the last person selected and going toward the first person selected. If you spelled the word correctly, you kept standing, but if you missed it, you sat down and became a spectator. Both parents and children participated. As they went back and forth the remaining participants left standing decreased as the words became more difficult. The competition continued until there was only one person left standing, and that person was the winner.

There was a foyer-like entrance to the schoolhouse with a hall leading to the rear classroom, which was the first and second grade. The stairs to the second floor also went off the foyer about ten feet inside the single hinged front door. There was a small porch on the front center of the building for the main entrance. The third, fourth and fifth grades were in one room, and the sixth and seventh grades in the third room. The principal taught the sixth and seventh grades and hygiene and math for the fifth grade.

The schoolhouse also had a large bell that was rung to start the school day and to start and end lunch hour and the two fifteen-minute recesses. If the bell rope was pulled too hard, the bell could turn completely over. Someone would have to go up in the belfry and correctly position the rope for proper operation.

Coal stoves in each room and in the auditorium provided heat in cold weather and each room had windows that were opened to ventilate the building in the warm months. There was a single light in each room and several in the auditorium. The wood and coal were stored under the schoolhouse.

An older student was hired by the teachers to clean the classrooms each day and build fires during cold weather. The student would go to school no later than six a.m. so that the rooms would be warm before classes started. He cleaned the school in the mornings while the building was heating. He was paid about three dollars a month for this work.

The schoolyard was about four acres and square in shape with the schoolhouse sitting near one of the front corners. A well was located about twenty feet in front of and off to the side of the schoolhouse. This was a deep well and you pumped the water into individual cups for the students. Each person usually had his or her own cup. I frequently left mine on the top of the well plunger. The rim of the cup was always beat up because the rack and sector gear of the pump would just catch the rim of the cup if the handle was raised high. The handle was straight with a steel ball in the end and about three to four feet long. You could hold your hand over the normal pump outlet and force water out the vent hole. The water surged upward and of course we would try to see who could pump it the highest. It could go about as high as the roof but this was never done if there was a teacher around. If one was careless and got caught, discipline followed.

The boys' outhouse was located in the diagonally opposite corner of the schoolyard from the schoolhouse, and the girls' was near and sort of behind the schoolhouse.

The horse stable was at the front corner of the school ground opposite the schoolhouse. The stable was adequate for about eight horses, which was more space than necessary when I attended the school. Uncle Tom's children drove a horse (Buster) and surrey and several other students sometimes rode horses to school. March and Ray Dellinger rode Arabian horses to school, which were the only Arabian horses I remember. Each owner had to bring his own feed and bedding and water the horses at noon.

We walked to grade school every year but one because we lived only one and one half miles from school by the road. The road itself was part macadam and part gravel. The one year we did not walk to school, we rode with one of the teachers, Miss Bowman (no relation), because Dick had a bad knee. I remember our route well. There was a swinging bridge over the one small stream. We usually did not use the bridge; instead we jumped from rock to rock at a narrow spot to get across the creek and once in a while we would fall in. The swinging bridge was usable during normal and relatively small rains and snows, but each end of the bridge could be flooded during heavy rains.

During dry weather we would take a shortcut to school through the fields. We either climbed over the fences or opened gates as we walked. I cannot remember ever tearing our clothes on the fences or leaving a gate open. The fences were mostly wire fences with one string of barbed wire on top. There was at least one rail fence depending on the field route taken. There were about five fences to cross on the route to and from school. There were only two on one route we sometimes took.

There was a cross cut on a limestone rock in the Bowman's pasture field. We talked about what might be under this rock and speculated that it could even have been an Indian grave, but no one ever dug under the rock to see what was actually there, so it is still a mystery.

Of course we played along the way both to and from school. Throwing rocks, chewing Life Everlasting (rabbit) tobacco, a plant which grows in the fields and, infrequently, there would be a fight, as can easily happen with boys.

I attended preschool for two or three days before the official commencement of first grade, which was somewhat customary. I went to the primary room the first day and sat with Aquilla, a boy one or two years older. I could read some and he insisted that I read, but after a while I thought, "Enough is enough," and when lunch hour was over, I went into my older brother Alden's room. The children, one at a time, would give me a pencil to take to Miss Cline, the teacher, to be peeked, as there were no pencil sharpeners in the school. This continued off and on all day and also the second day. My mother found out that I was not staying in the primary room, and this ended my "formal" preschool training.

The first day of school each year was always an exciting day because we had not seen many of our schoolmates since school closed for the summer. This first day we walked to the Eckard's Store to be weighed and again the last day of the school year. The most exciting part of the first day was burning off the school yard. The schoolyard was mowed about two weeks before school commenced in September. We raked the dry grass into piles and wind rows and then set the dry grass on fire. We cut limbs off the pine trees and used these limbs to keep the fire under control. The schoolyard activity kept the grass under control during the school year.

Mr. John Foltz's general store was about a half mile from the school. If we had a penny or more we would sometimes go to his store at noon for treats. Big suckers were a penny apiece as were small Baby Ruth candy bars. Licorice was also a favorite and you got two or three long sticks for a penny. I do not remember us spending more than a penny or two on any one day.

The principal, Mr. Lewis Dellinger, taught the fifth grade math and hygiene. He was a good teacher and was in control of all aspects of the school. I remember that in hygiene he told us to brush our tongue when we brushed our teeth to prevent bad breath. All of our teachers were capable nice people and both students and parents respected them.

We never had a teacher we did not like. On one occasion we overheard one of the teachers say to another teacher that she would not take seventy-five dollars for her camera. The second teacher asked if that was because of the children's pictures she had on film. The answer was, "No, I have my monthly paycheck in the back of the camera." Apparently, money has always been an important item, even for a dedicated school teacher.

The only time I was the teacher's "pet" was in my first grade. I would sit on Miss Harpine's lap occasionally and everyone considered me her pet. Discipline was strict but I don't think I got "caught" at anything serious enough to get physical discipline. Each teacher had switches, a ruler, etc. to deal the more serious discipline. We were never sent out of the room unless it was to go to the principal's office for some infraction. I was sent there only once and of course I denied the charge, but he knew I was guilty. I do not know if I improved or if I just never got caught again, but I suspect the latter. This was what discipline is all about, you learn.

The major games we played at grade school were ball games. Town ball was the ball game we usually played but we also played dodge ball and paddle cat. I do not remember the details of paddle cat. The town ball diamond was similar to a baseball diamond. A bat and ball was all the equipment needed. We used whatever ball was available, such as hard rubber dog balls, tennis balls, and even golf balls. The hard rubber dog balls were the favorite. A pitcher, a catcher, three outfielders, three infielders and a rover made up the team.

We chose up sides using a bat to determine which team leader got the first pick, with the best players picked first. The first pick was made by the team leader whose grip was nearest the handle end of the bat. The person's grip had to be strong enough to throw the bat over the person's head. No "crow picking" was allowed. Crow picking was reaching down on the end of the bat and grasping it with the thumb and fingers. The ball was pitched underhanded and passed over the plate area without striking the ground. The catcher stood far enough behind the batter to catch an unhit pitch on first bounce.

Three strikes constituted an out. Each person was entitled to one out each inning. If you were the only one not out and you got on base you used a substitute runner. After you hit the ball you could be put out in two ways. The first way was for your ball to be caught on a fly or first bounce. The second way was to have the ball thrown across the baseline between the runner and the next base he was running to. Backup for the thrown ball was important to keep other runners from advancing. The bats were round and usually homemade, using a draw knife to shape the bat. Occasionally someone would bring a store-bought bat. There were no gloves worn and a long fly ball to outfield would sting, especially if you were playing with a golf ball.

I know we played other games but I do not remember them. Girls played town ball also but on a separate smaller diamond. Almost everyone would play some game at recess and lunch hour except when a player had a romance going. That would take priority over other games but most of these did not last long. They always flourished just before the night league school programs such as Halloween and Christmas. Big plans were made for these nights, but to the best of my knowledge none of those plans came to fruition.

Some quite humorous things happened in grade school, or at least they seem humorous now. Many of the boys trapped for rabbits, foxes, possums, muskrats or skunks in the winter months. One cold school morning after we had gone inside we began to smell skunk. It quickly became stronger as Leon Fultz's clothes got warm. Leon had gone to check his traps and had caught two skunks, which he killed. He tied them on the end of a pole, put the pole over his shoulder, and took them home. This was not an unusual occurrence; however, this morning the skunks slid down the pole and lay against his back. He was sent home, the window opened, a brief recess given and classes resumed with the skunk odor still in the classroom!

Another time, J.R. Foltz came to school feeling sick. The teacher put him up near the stove, since he must have been chilly. By noon, he was covered with spots, and about twenty of the thirty children in that room got the measles from J.R.! So you see, most people were unselfish, even to the sharing of the measles.

One of the most memorable funny incidents during our years at Hamburg Grade School involved Buddy, who was in the same class as I, and his older neighbor, Joe Long. Joe had a metal detector which he used to locate metal underground, always expecting the metal to be valuable. Everyone likes to play jokes, especially on their friends. Buddy filled a teakettle with copper and other metal and buried the kettle. The next time Buddy went with Joe to hunt for buried treasure he maneuvered Joe to the area where he had buried the kettle. Sure enough, the detector signaled a "find." They dug the dirt away from the kettle. Buddy picked up the kettle and ran down through the field. Joe was right behind him yelling "half mine, Buddy, half mine!" Of course, Buddy was known as "Half Mine" for years to come.

There were also some very sad times. The greatest tragedy occurred when one of our classmates climbed an electric utility pole, came in contact with a bare wire, and was electrocuted. I remember no general or specific counseling relative to this tragedy; we just "handled it."

## Triplett High School

I began attending Triplett High School at Mt. Jackson in September, 1938. Triplett, one of five high schools in Shenandoah County, was five miles from home and was relatively big, so it was quite a transition to adapt from a three-room grade school to a high school where one changed rooms almost every class period. We adapted easily to this and paid little attention to the "town clique" in the school. We just seemed to regard everyone like everyone else, and got along fine.

The first year we rode with Uncle Tom to high school. He took several of his children, a schoolteacher, Dick and me. My uncle was not the world's safest driver and after that year I figured I had used up much of my luck, so in the future I had better be especially careful. He never put his arm out the window to give a turn signal and paid little attention at the railroad track or anywhere else, for that matter. But he never had an accident as far as I know.

Since I didn't recognize one song from another and had no acting ability, I did not participate in school activities such as Glee Club or class plays. These entailed rehearsals after school and if I had participated, I may have had to walk the five miles home. As active as I was, that prospect seemed to be a waste of my time. Besides, we had work to do at home after school.

There were fewer fights in high school, but they did occur. The last one I remember was in my second year when someone was picking on a smaller boy on our team so we quickly came to an "understanding." Our principal was very strict and a tough disciplinarian. My eye was getting quite black by the time I went to his math class.

He said, "Elmore Bowman, what happened to your eye?" I said, "Something hit me." He never questioned me as to whose fist it was. He probably thought I had had punishment enough already.

We had the largest graduation class in the history of the school, graduating 49! We had started with 80 freshmen. I was in the upper ten percent of the class academically. My mother expected me to do better, but I remember no great pressure relative to this. Maybe we were not smart enough to know what great stress we were under. The students who did the best academically were the ones whose parents got across to them how important it was to take meaningful courses and excel in them. Agriculture and Shop were two basic courses that were considered to be relatively easy. I did not take these because my father said he would teach me what I needed to know about the farm and that I should take more difficult courses. This was excellent guidance.

**Figure 15**
Hamburg Three-Room Grade School

**Figure 16**
Triplett High School, Mt. Jackson, Virginia

**Figure 17**
Twyman Elmore As High School Senior, Age 16

## Chapter Twelve

## MEDICAL CARE

The two hospitals in the Shenandoah area were located at Harrisonburg, thirty miles south, and at Winchester, forty miles north. Each town in Shenandoah County had one or more doctors and some small communities, such as Conicville, had one. Dr. Downey, who practiced in Edinburg, five miles from our home, was our family doctor. He was the only doctor I ever went to until I left home. We were very fortunate that we had no illness requiring special treatment by other doctors. We always referred to going to see "our friend" when it was necessary to see Dr. Downey.

My immediate family was blessed with good health. Of course, the good health of us boys was attributable to having the right mother and father. Our family thought Dr. Downey was the best doctor in the world. He had a larger practice when he was 70 than when he was 30, rnainly due to having better mobility in an automobile in the later years than by horse and buggy in the earlier years. An office visit was about $1 and a house call about $3. We went to his Edinburg office whenever practical, and the only time I remember him coming to our house to see me was when I was ill with a severe case of scarlet fever.

All three of us Bowman boys were born at home. Alden and I were born at our first home, the tenant house owned by Grandpa Bowman, and Dick was born in the home that Mother and Dad built in 1925. My mother had a midwife in addition to the general care of Dr. Downey for the birth of each of us boys. The births were normal for that day and time, and no special care was required. The midwife who attended my mother when I was born suggested the name "Twyman," and the "Elmore" was a tribute to Reverend Elmore. Now I answer to Twyman, Elmore, Mo, Bo and most frequently, Ty.

Mother was hospitalized for a few days on one occasion, whereas Dad never had a hospital stay. However, Dad had back trouble, and every now and then would go to the chiropractor at Harrisonburg. When the pain would get so great that he felt he could not properly function, he would say, "Folks, tomorrow I will go to Harrisonburg to my punching doctor." Those chiropractor visits always seemed to help.

Alden and Dick had the usual childhood diseases, such as measles, whooping cough, and mumps. I had none of these childhood diseases even though I honestly tried to get them because the prevailing view was that the younger one was when he got them, the less chance of having complications, particularly from the mumps. So we all deliberately played together and drank out of the same cup when one of my brothers had such a disease. If any of our friends got one of these diseases, we would go visit them, giving us more exposure. When we came home from the visit my mother would ask us if we went in the room and sat near the sick child. If our answer was "No" we were sent back for a "real" visit.

The only one of us who had surgery was Dick, and this was to remove his tonsils. He was, unknowingly, a free bleeder and had to be returned to the operating room twice after the original surgery. The first time, to have his vessels retied, but the second time they were found to be all right, and needed no further tying.

I had scarlet fever in 1939, and Dr. Downey made a house call to treat me on Christmas morning. He nailed up the "QUARANTINE" sign at our house as he left. We were quarantined for two or three weeks. I really gave the family a never-to-be-forgotten Christmas present that year! No one else in the family or neighborhood caught scarlet fever from me. This was mostly because of the excellent nurse I had, my mother. She took care of me 24 hours a day and for about five of those days I was "out-of-my-head." They were unable to determine where I was exposed, since there were no known cases of scarlet fever anywhere around. The doctor's theory was that I caught it from someone who had such a mild case that they never knew they had it, and that was why it was so severe on me. My ears were "gathered" (infected) for two weeks, but my hearing appeared to be unaffected by the ear infection.

Our other illnesses were minor and we treated them with home remedies. We took a teaspoon of sugar saturated with coal oil (kerosene) for coughs. Mustard plasters or Vick's on our chest were to break up chest colds. We would "roast" our feet before going to bed at night to help ward off colds, I think. We would sit around the stove with the bottoms of our feet near the stove for 15 minutes or so, letting our feet get as hot as we could stand them. Warts were removed by tying a thread tightly around the wart, putting on a new, tighter thread every day or so until the wart died and came off. Of course, Castor oil was the predominant laxative. The first tablespoon of Castor oil was not so bad, but the second one was about all we could tolerate. Iodine and Mercurochrome were always put on open scratches and cuts to sterilize the wound, followed later by salves to promote healing.

The Raleigh and Watkins drummers periodically came by selling medical supplies such as salves, tonics, pills, etc. Oscar Gochenour was the Raleigh man and I can remember him carrying large quantities of medication in his coat and pants pockets. It was always amazing to see him continually pull bottles, cans and jars of stuff out of his pockets. I do not remember the Watkins man, so he must not have been as much of a character as the Raleigh man.

Dr. Wunder, located at Woodstock, was our dentist during our early years; then we all went to Dr. Martin at nearby Mt. Jackson when he set up practice there. Dr. Martin probably had more influence on me than anyone else other than my mother and father, particularly during my high school years. He shared his thoughts and experiences with me and helped motivate me. He probably had a greater positive impact on people in the community than any other single individual. I will always be extremely grateful for all that he did for me in so many ways. His hard work and caring nature saved my teeth, for my teeth were very prone to need fillings. From my early teens to the mid-20s, I probably averaged 15-20 fillings per year, but I never had to have a tooth removed.

Mother procrastinated going to the dentist so that when she did go, she really needed work badly. The day the Nelson Theater burned was one of those times she went to see Dr. Martin. He would work on her teeth and then they would watch the fire, and then back to the teeth. She had 16 teeth filled that day. Father left home one morning in late summer of 1939 and told no one where he was going. He went by the Lohr's watermelon patch, bought eight watermelons, went by the store, bought two packs of cigarettes (he smoked a crooked stem pipe), and then went to see Dr. Martin. Dr. Martin pulled all his teeth and he drove back home. My mother fussed a tad at him for that escapade. Alden had good hard teeth, whereas Dick and I had soft teeth that were prone to decay. We probably took a half-gallon of chocolate tasting pills to harden our teeth, but I doubt that they helped.

Dr. Martin was a favorite of many, many people and could joke and tell jokes with the best. Someone from out of town stopped and asked one of our townspeople where Dr. Martin's office was located. He said, "Turn right at the Atlantic station and stop at the house that has jawbones lying in the front yard." This is typical of the sense of humor between people who like to kid others. Dr. Martin and his wife had a greater positive influence on other people than anyone I know, as I have already stated.

Mr. Frank Dinges, the druggist at Edinburg, was sort of a second doctor to us. He had many concoctions that he put together for various ailments. One of them was petroleum iodine, which contained iodine, oils, and who knows what else. We used it on cuts to prevent infection and also for healing purposes. He also served ice cream and sodas, and now and then we would be treated to one or the other. The whole family admired and depended on him for all our medical needs, except when we needed to go to Dr. Downey.

We had the usual and some unusual accidents as boys. Typical accidents were stumping a toe when going barefooted, cuts on our hands, legs, arms and feet, stepping on nails (danger of blood poison since most exposed nails were rusty). Mother often told the story of an especially bad day that I do not remember: When I was about two years old, I walked up behind Alden, who was hoeing in the garden. He swung the hoe over his head to get a heavy stroke, and the hoe split one of my eyebrows. Mother stopped the bleeding, bandaged my eye, and turned me loose. My father was stapling the fence using a hatchet to drive the staples. I walked up behind him without him knowing it, and as he drew back the hatchet to hit the staple, he split my upper lip! I was not noted for being a fast learner.

## Chapter Thirteen

# TRAVEL AND TRANSPORTATION

The major mode of travel and transportation was the automobile, as far as our immediate family was concerned. There was still some horse-drawn transportation activity during the early part of my childhood that I observed but was never a participant.

Wagons pulled by either one horse or two horses were needed to haul products to the mill or to other markets. The products were hay, corn, barley and wheat, most of which was taken to the mill for sale. Some of this grain was ground and cracked and brought back to the farm to feed the animals. Wheat was ground into flour for home use. The spring wagon was used to haul relatively small quantities, such as a half-ton, and the larger "road wagon" was used for greater quantities. The buggy was used for hauling very small quantities, such as groceries, hardware, parts taken to the blacksmith for repair, etc. Single-person trips such as a visit and business were frequently traveled on horseback. Women usually rode sidesaddle rather than the conventional saddle.

One or two horses pulled the spring wagon. The wagon-bed was high off the ground and about six feet wide, twelve feet long, and fifteen inches deep, and supported on springs. The single seat was the full width of the wagon-bed and rested on the two sides of the bed. This permitted the entire bed to be loaded, and the seat was removable for easy loading and unloading. The seat was mounted on a separate set of springs sized to give some degree of comfort over the rough roads. Three people could sit side by side on this seat with one person driving the horse or horses using check lines. The spring wagon had a handbrake to use going downhill so the horse did not have to hold the wagon from going too fast.

The "road wagon" was the same wagon that was used in the fields to haul hay, wheat, and barley. The hay and grain crane was removed and a wagon-bed placed on the wagon chassis. The wagon-bed was shorter than the crane so the coupling pole which connected the front-end assembly to the rear-end assembly, was shortened. This was simply done by pulling one metal pin and rolling the rear wheels forward to the desired position and reinserting the pin. The bed was about six feet wide, 18 feet long, and two feet deep. Sideboards were put on top of the bed to increase the bed capacity. The wagon had brakes on the two rear wheels that had to be set while standing on the ground. This necessitated stopping before starting down the hill to set the brake unless someone was walking beside the wagon. The brake could be applied much more effectively if someone was walking beside the wagon, but this required two men instead of just one.

The buggy was used for more stylish transportation or when only very small amounts of cargo were to be handled, such as one or two hundred pounds. The buggy could seat two adults in the seat with two children behind the seat facing backwards if there was no cargo. The buggy wheels were wood-spoked wheels with either steel rims or steel rims with rubber tires. The rubber tires were an extra cost item much as today's extras are on automobiles. The buggy top usually folded down and it also had various types of side, front and rear curtains for inclement weather. It was pulled with one horse and had no braking system; therefore, the horse had to hold the buggy back when going downhill.

The buggy body was supported on the axles with transverse leaf springs. This type spring is still referred to as a buggy spring and was used on many of the early automobiles. In fact, Ford did not change over until the 1949 model. Buggy sales agencies were set up similar to the automobile dealerships of today. The type top, curtains, coats of paint, trim, wheels and tires, suspension, etc. all were factors in the price. The buckboard was essentially a buggy with no top.

The surrey was the family vehicle and had either two or three transverse seats and could accommodate six or nine people, respectively. The running gear was essentially the same as the buggy, only larger. The top normally did not fold down and it may have various arrangements of side, front and rear side coverings. Uncle Tom had a surrey that his many children used to drive to Hamburg School pulled by the horse, Buster. The horse was stabled at the school during the day.

There was a two-wheeled vehicle, the "studhorse" cart, which the studhorse owner drove around to the farms for the stud horse to service eligible mares. This cart had a spring seat with only a small rim around it to keep the driver from sliding off. (Mr. Holler gave us boys one of these carts, which we trained our pet cow to pull.) The purpose for breeding the mare was to raise the colt to a full-grown horse for the farmer's use or for him to sell for profit. Horses were sold and traded back then much as automobiles are today.

The first automobile that my father and mother had was a Model T Ford which they used until they bought a new 1928 Model A Ford. He may have had the Model T before they married and used it for part of his courting days. I do not remember the Model T except that it was discarded on the junk machinery rock at my grandparents'. The Model A was a blue two-door car and was used for both work and pleasure.

My father made a flat box to extend about three feet beyond the spare tire and the full width of the car. This box could be put on or taken off in a minute as no screws or bolts were used for mounting. The major purpose of the box was to haul gasoline, oil and tools to the thresher and baler since the car had no trunk. The box held six five-gallon cans of gasoline or oil, which was more than adequate for one day's work.

The next family car was a blue 1937 four-door Dodge, purchased by Uncle Harry on January 4, 1938, in New York City at the year-end closeout sale for about $700. Many of our neighbors came by to look the car over, for there were few new cars bought in the community. The car had a heater but no defroster or radio. My father had a defroster installed after a trip to Harper's Ferry during which Uncle Claude had to wipe the inside of the windshield all the way there and back. A radio was never installed. The battery was located under the front seat. The tires were Cooper and they all split between the treads just when tires became rationed during World War II. The Dodge lasted until about 1952, and all three of us boys used it for part of our dating careers.

The Model A was still used as the work car after we bought the Dodge. The differential of the Model A became quite noisy; in fact we could hear it coming almost a half-mile away. We bought a used International pickup for work duty and sold the Model A for $10 or $15.

There were many Model T's on the road during the late 20's and early 30's. Our closest neighbor, Mr. Ernest, had a Model T, but he never completely mastered it. His garage was about 100 yards from the road. My brother and I would watch him leave in the morning and we would guess how many jumps it would make from the garage to the road, with six to ten being the usual. Uncle Wib also had a Model T, which he drove very well.

The family would get together and go on picnics several times during the summer using this car. One summer we went to "Adam's Hole," which was at the top of a very steep hill with a stream flowing out of the mountain. The Model T would not pull the hill going forward, so Uncle Wib backed his car up the hill so that the gravity feed fuel tank would be above the carburator.

Our normal transportation to grade school was walking, since it was only one and one-half miles. My father or a neighbor would drive us to school if the weather was very bad and they were not working. Mother never drove. Dick had a bad knee one year, so we both rode with a teacher, Miss Ruth Bowman, that year only. I rode to Triplett High School during the first year with Uncle Tom, who was taking two of his children there also. Uncle Tom was not the greatest driver, but he never had an accident. He would blow the horn at the railroad crossing and give his turning hand signals without rolling down the car window, but we never had a wreck! A school bus came by our home in my second year, so I rode the bus until I graduated. The distance was five miles to the high school. If you missed the bus, you had to walk, which further advanced your education.

The roads and highways were maintained by the State. However, roads to private homes were maintained by the homeowner or homeowners. The lane to my father's home place was one half-mile and maintained by them alone. There was a lane to Uncle John's, Uncle Tom's, and Mr. Sam's home, which was maintained by all three of them. I remember looking toward Uncle Tom's one morning and seeing his car parked in the lane. My father said that Sam and Linden had probably run out of gas on their way home from an evening party. They could not get the car weaned so it would run without gas.

Heavy snows were a problem both due to the depth of the snow and the drifting of the snow. Frequently, somewhere along the road the roadbed would be lower than the surrounding land, and the snow would drift over if there was much wind. As the snow blew across the road, it would drop onto the road and remain there similar to the way it would do if it blew across a ditch. If the snow melted just a little a crust would form on the snow that prevented the snow from blowing.

My father and uncle built a snowplow which was about fifteen feet long and ten or twelve feet wide. It was triangular-shaped with the smallest angle being the front end. Three horses would be hooked to the plow. The plow was weighted down with steel weights and up to six people. This type plow was far from ideal since there was little capability to steer it as it followed along behind the horses. The snow was usually uneven due to drifting, which would cause the plow to take the course of least resistance. The men would move around on the plow so as to provide some steerage power. They would periodically shovel the deep snow partially away so that the plow could remove the remainder. The plow was pulled through the field parallel to the road and upwind of the road so as to form the equivalent of a snow fence.

This would cause the blown snow to drift onto the plowed path in the field before it got to the road.

There was also bus and train service. The Greyhound bus carried passengers up and down the valley on U.S. 11. It also carried small quantities of cargo. The first bus trip I ever took was from Washington, D.C., to Mt. Jackson, when I visited at Uncle Claude's for a week. A highlight of that visit was seeing the parade given "Wrong Way Corrigan" with my cousin Maggie. Maggie knew the route, so we moved around and saw him at three or four locations.

Another bus trip I took was when Aunt Mae took me to New York City for a week of sightseeing. Uncle Harry and Aunt Katherine lived there while Uncle Harry's military assignment was in New York City. Aunt Mae, Uncle Harry and Aunt Katherine showed me what I thought must have been all of New York City, including the circus. I particularly remember the circus because when we got there, Aunt Katherine said, "Just smell the circus." Uncle Harry replied, "That's not what I smell." We took in stage shows as well as the typical city sights.

The railroad ran up and down the valley carrying passengers, mail and freight. The freight included hogs, cattle and sheep, as well as other merchandise. My father often told of the train crash at Narrow Passage when the high bridge collapsed. The train was loaded with cattle, most of which were seriously injured or killed. He heard the noise from the crash at his home, which was about five miles away. Passenger service was discontinued when I was very young, and the mail service about 1938. The train still runs today, and is frequently referred to as "Try Train," that is, it will try today and if it doesn't make it will try again tomorrow!

Even during the late 1930's, much cargo was carried up and down the valley by tractor-trailer trucks such as The Mason-Dixon Line. Traveling route 11 could seem like being in a tunnel because of so many trucks going each way. The Route 11 traffic would be routed past our house if the Shenandoah River flooded over Route 11 at Redbanks. The road would give way under the weight of the trucks as they passed, which would ruin the road surface in a very short time.

## Chapter Fourteen

# CLOTHING

Clothing was never of interest to us at any time except when we went from short pants to long pants. The attire for most of the boys in grade school was bib overall and shirt with whatever sweaters and coats we needed during cool and cold weather. My mother, who was quite a good seamstress, made the shirts and summer underwear. She had a treadle "New Home" sewing machine that she used to make new clothes and alter old clothes. The next child down the line wore the outgrown clothes; however, most of our clothes were completely worn out before they were outgrown. This was because we had few clothes and therefore they were worn often. At any given time we probably had two pairs of overalls for school, one to wear and one in the wash. We put on older clothes as soon as we got home from school before doing the evening chores to increase the life of the school clothes.

Mother usually did the laundry on Mondays, but she was not as fanatical about washing on Mondays as some of our neighbors were. My father's clothes were very dirty and greasy from working around the machinery. Three boys' dirty clothes were also no snap to get clean. The clothes-washing process was somewhat different for the colored dirty clothes as compared to the white clothes. The dirty clothes were placed in a wash kettle and boiled to help get the dirt and grease out of the cloth. Mother also did the laundry for Mr. Dave Rinker, who worked for my father. Mr. Dave never married and lived alone. He often cut my father's hair and us three boys' hair at a cost of ten or fifteen cents each.

Homemade soap was the chief product used for washing clothes. Mother made the soap, including preparing the ingredients and boiling the soap. Soap was made of caustic soda, cracklings, lard, fat meat, etc. The caustic soda helped break down the other ingredients, and the wash kettle was used to cook it all into soap. This concoction was cooked for hours and hours and then left to cool naturally. The soap rose to the top and was a yellow-beige color. The layer of soap was three to four inches thick, depending on the overall depth of the cooking liquid. The black non-soap part settled to the bottom of the kettle, had a slurry-like viscosity and was referred to as lye. The soap was the consistency of today's soap but was not normally used for bathing or hand washing.

We helped Mother cut and trim the soap from the kettle. We buried the lye that was not saved for further use. The clothes were removed from the kettle and wrung out by hand. They were then put in a tub of hot soapy water and soaked. A scrub-board was used to hand scrub the clothes that had not come clean in the kettle or the tub soaking. The clothes were then rinsed and wrung out prior to hanging on the clothesline. The clotheslines were located in the pasture field, where the cows loved to walk underneath and make the clothes dirty again. So the cows had to be penned up when clothes were on the line. After we got electricity we bought a Voss washing machine, which normally sold for $80, for $40 on close out. The washer was a round tub with two rectangular tubs on legs and rollers.

Wet clothes dried quickly in the summer, but were sort of freeze-dried in the winter, so it took much longer in cold weather. Clothes were removed from the clotheslines, folded, placed in a washtub and brought into the house. The night before the clothes were to be ironed, they were unfolded, sprinkled with water, rolled up and placed back in the washtub. Then they were ironed on the kitchen table with flat irons heated on the wood-burning kitchen stove. Some of these irons had iron handles, which required a thick cloth holder to prevent burning the hands. The other type had removable wooden handles that were clamped to the flat iron before it was removed from the stove. My mother frequently used four irons, with three heating while one was being used.

The hot stove was comfortable in the winter as this heated the kitchen, but was uncomfortable in the hot summer days. My dog (Peggy) would lie under the stove until she got too hot, and then move under the kitchen table to cool off and then back under the stove again. This was a city dog and I think she was not too smart.

The transition from short pants to long pants for Sunday was a very significant step up the ladder. This occurred about age ten. Any clothes other than school, work and play clothes were considered "Sunday clothes" and got special care, however they also suffered from our activities. We had a two door Model (A) Ford and we frequently crawled in and out of the car through the rear window. One summer day I crawled out the car window, stood on the running board facing toward the rear of the car and stepped off while the car was still moving. I fell on my back on the macadam road in a puddle of melted tar. I learned quite a bit in several ways from that one experience. The tar never came out of the white short pants and shirt.

We altered our coats, pants, socks, shoes, and the like to extend their usefulness. My father had a last which he used to put soles and heels on our shoes. I don't remember having a store-bought shirt until I was well into high school but long-handled winter underwear was store-bought. Our parents paid particular attention to see that our shoes did not cramp our feet, which meant that most of our new shoes were larger than needed when bought. My father had problems with his feet, which he felt was largely due to wearing small shoes when he was a boy. Each generation always wants better for their children than they had, and our parents were no exception about things that really counted.

Straw hats were the head covers that we wore during the summer and toboggans were worn during the winter to keep our heads and ears warm. Straw hats were frequently used as defensive weapons against bumblebees, honeybees, wasps, etc. Straw hats were not made for use as weapons, and even a small amount of bee fighting would leave you with a severely damaged hat. Bee stings were normal happenings and I do not remember anyone getting sick from the stings, but they did hurt and were a nuisance. Alden got stung about three times on his upper lip by wasps while climbing over a fence. We told him he looked like a half Ubanga.

The first day of May was a big day when we were small because that was the first day we were allowed to go barefooted. We liked this and it also saved shoes and socks. There were thistles, sand briers, stubbles, sharp rocks, etc. which had to be avoided or pay the price. Stepping on nails was also dangerous because they were always rusty and the wound would become infected. Two other hazards were stumped toes and cow itch. Stumped toes were caused by hitting your toe on a rock, board, etc. tearing the end of the toe. I am not sure what caused cow itch, but the toes would break open on the underside, bleed and itch. We quit going barefoot when we went back to school in the fall. We would walk over rough surfaces such as gravel to "show off" how tough our feet were when we were barefoot.

We wore better-looking clothes to high school but serviceability was more important than looks. Corduroy was one of the tougher materials for boys' pants, and toughness was necessary for playing football, softball, etc. We wore ties to school on the day pictures were to be taken, but seldom did otherwise. However, ties were part of our "Sunday clothes." We dressed to suit the weather with overcoats in the winter, raincoats for rain, and rubbers for rain and snow. Knee boots, hip boots, leggings and four-buckle arctics were worn on special occasions such as deep snow and high waters.

The above describes what boys wore and does not address what girls wore, largely because I have almost no recollection of the girls' attire. I think they wore dresses, skirts, blouses, sweaters, coats and overshoes of one kind or another. We all dressed for the temperature, the weather and to look presentable. There were few "clotheshorses" among our family and friends.

## Chapter Fifteen

# SOCIALIZING

Our socializing consisted of visiting friends and relatives and attending school, picnics, fire carnivals and lawn parties, band reunion, apple blossom festival, church, belsnickeling (described later), the county fair, etc. Some of these activities had dual benefits, such as school and church.

We visited our grandmothers more than anyone else. Grandmother Dellinger lived five miles away and we usually had at least a weekly visit with her. Grandmother Bowman lived only one half mile away, so our visits to see her were more frequent and casual, particularly for us boys, who saw her during our play and our work at her farm. We always visited Uncle Wib, Aunt Stella, and Charles each time we visited Grandmother Dellinger, because they lived near her. We visited the relatives in Ohio twice, and Uncle Claude, Aunt Celia, Claude Jr., and Maggie in Washington a few times.

The Ohio relatives and Uncle Claude visited us frequently, for there were so many friends and relatives for them to see as compared to us making an Ohio or a Washington visit. Mr. Norman and Mrs. Daisy Stoner were my parents' closest friends and we visited back and forth frequently. They had no children but always a cat, which was like part of their family. We also visited back and forth with our neighbors and other relatives. Mrs. Daisy gave Mother an organ, which was always in our parlor and played by my mother.

School programs, spelling bees and school league were further socializing events. We would usually invite the grade school teachers to dinner at our house about once a year. The Sunday school service, church programs and church picnics were special occasions we looked forward to. The minister and his family were also invited for dinner about once a year at our home. The presence of the school teacher and the minister's family in the house called for our best behavior. We must have passed muster because I cannot remember a case that our behavior was a subject for uncomplimentary discussion after the guests had left. We would have family picnics several times each summer with different members of the families. The largest was the Bowman Reunion, which was frequently held at Endless Caverns.

Fire carnivals and lawn parties were similar events except that the fire carnival in each town lasted several nights. The purpose of a fire carnival was to raise money to help support the volunteer fire company. Food and drinks were sold, and there were parades and games such as bingo, baseballs and milk bottles, and coin tossing. Dick and I entered the Mt. Jackson Fire Carnival parade with our trained cow pulling a buggy. We drove the cow with check lines and a bridle and bit just the same way we would have a horse. People told us we could not use a bit in a cow's mouth, as the cow would lose its cud. We disabused them of that notion, because we never had a problem, so we put their admonition down as another "old wives' tale."

The band reunion was of special interest to the Bowman family, since it was held about one half mile from our home in Mr. Clanahan's woods. Bands would come from many communities and the band concerts were a major attraction. They had ice cream, hot dogs, pies, cakes, etc. to sell as well as a few games. The cakewalk was always popular. Couples would walk around the bandstand while the band played. Everyone stopped walking when the band stopped playing, and the couple nearest the cake won. The band stopped at random times and not necessarily at the end of a number.

Jim, a local vagabond, came to visit us at each band reunion so that he could attend the band reunion each day. Jim traveled throughout the community, spending a few days here and there. He came to our house several times a year, and my mother treated him very well. He was quite a hearty eater. I remember one Sunday when he was there. We had so much company for dinner that there were two sittings for the adults, plus one for the children. Jim ate at the first sitting, did not get up, and ate again at the second sitting! He was very hard of hearing, so he used a hearing aid. The hearing aid consisted of an oil can with the bottom cut out. It looked like a funnel with a small discharge pipe. He placed the small pipe in his ear and one spoke into the large end. It always worked because there were no batteries to go bad.

Belsnickeling was also quite popular during the Christmas holiday period. Families and/or groups of people would get together, put on costumes and visit in the homes. A belsnickeler whose identity was guessed had to remove the head covering. Some of the costumes were extremely fascinating, and the acting and disguising of voices were well done. The belsnickelers were given cookies, cakes, cider, coffee, candy, etc. before they left. It was a fine time for everyone involved.

The county fair was also a time for meeting and visiting people you may see from far and near. The fair ran from Tuesday through Saturday, with Tuesday being children's day. Harness races were held every day and free acts were held each afternoon and night. These could all be better seen from the grandstand. It cost to get in the grandstand, so we never sat there. Many businesses, such as farm machine sales, insurance sales, and automobile sales, had displays that they hoped would attract business. The poultry exhibit was quite large, as well as the canned goods, vegetable and farm products. The largest exhibits were the farm animals, which included horses, cattle, hogs, sheep, and there were many categories of each of these. The Four-H Clubs were also quite active. Everything we did and everywhere we went was, to a certain extent, a socializing event.

The annual Apple Blossom Festival, held in Winchester, was an event we anticipated and we went to several times. One year when the Mt. Jackson band was in the parade, my father was quite noticeable. It was not his playing the slide trombone, but that he was the only bareheaded band member in the entire parade. I do not remember why he did not have a hat unless it was that the band did not own enough.

Halloween pranks were also a form of socializing and covered a wide range of mischief. The Halloweeners would put buggies up on top of farm buildings by taking them apart on the ground and reassembling them on top of the building. It's amazing how ingenious people become while being mischievous. Another prank was to push over corn shocks. They did this to Uncle John, but he found out who was involved, rounded the boys up on Saturday, and had them shuck all the corn they pushed over. That was the last time I remember seeing that prank. Lifting gates off hinges and moving things such as machinery were more Halloween pranks. There was no "trick or treat," only "tricks."

Wiener roasts were popular and enjoyed by everyone. My grandmother had a wiener roast and a fire was built on a large limestone rock. The fire got the rock so hot that the rock exploded, knocking the hot dogs off the sticks and spraying the roasters with fire and ashes. They never made that mistake again. Cake, cookies and ice cream were also served at the wiener roasts.

We took few pictures, as cameras, film and film development money could be used for more essential items. My parents did get us a new box camera from Sears, Roebuck for $2.10, but we bought and used film sparingly, so we have few pictures of us as children.

After a couple married and returned to live with one of their families or live on their own, they were subject to a "Belling." At a specific time, unknown to the couple, family and friends show up and serenade the couple. Everyone brought their loudest noisemaker so that the overall volume would be great. The noise level was always high and would last for an hour or so, until the couple came out and greeted the uninvited guests. Infrequently, a couple would slip out of the house unobserved and hide out until the "guests" left. The guests usually came back again and did the job right. The belling was expected and the couple normally came out to greet the guests and served some kind of refreshments.

Noise was made by singing, yelling, shooting shotguns, setting off firecrackers, hammering on wash tubs and by doing anything else one could think of to make a racket. One of the most penetrating noisemakers was for someone to strike a large circular saw with a hammer or mall while two people loosely held the saw in a non-restricted manner. The blade was very hard steel, about three feet in diameter, and would ring and ring after each blow.

Sitting up with the dead was another ritual in vogue during my youth. Funeral homes were not used for the ritual itself, but would prepare the deceased for burial, place the body in the casket, and then return the casket and body to the family's home for the sitting ritual. The deceased would be placed in the family parlor, and family and friends would take turns sitting in the room with the body. Refreshments were served to the sitters. Sitting with the dead was continuous ritual from the time of death until burial, and was a time to pay respect to the deceased and to socialize with family and friends. Later, the funeral home would officiate at the funeral and the burial.

"Poundings" were held when neighbors wanted to help or welcome someone. Everyone met at the family residence and brought a gift, usually something useful. One frequently gave a pound of this or a pound of that as well as gifts such as clothing, tools, etc., depending on the reason for the pounding. These were often done following a home fire, a family down-on-their-luck, a new person in the community such as a minister, etc., and was a helpful method of socializing.

At some point in high school each of us boys became interested in girls. I met someone special when I was sixteen. I had limited access to an automobile because both Alden and I used the family car. Because it was wartime, gas was rationed and the family was only allotted three gallons of gas per week. Consequently, I often walked to my date's house, and we would walk to visit family and friends together. I have many fond memories of those times.

Chapter Sixteen

## FEARS, DANGERS AND CONCERNS

Fire has probably always engendered the greatest fear in anyone who lives in a rural area such as the Shenandoah Valley, prompting a need for vigilance day and night. Homes could be many miles from the nearest volunteer fire company or there may be essentially no water with which to fight the fire. Most of the water supplies had a flow of only a few gallons per minute, which is adequate to water stock and for other normal uses but is inadequate to fight a fire. A family and/or all of their possessions may be wiped out in a matter of minutes from fire. I remember when I was only a few years old, Mrs. Effie Wolfe was visiting in our home one evening. As she was leaving, we noticed a fire off in the distance. She said that the fire may be her home, and it was. This left a lasting impression on us children, as we knew this could happen to anyone.

We were also aware of the danger presented by the machinery that our father used every day, any one of which could cause serious injury or death in a careless moment. The feeder belt and feeder knives on a threshing machine would hack a person to death in seconds if he were to fall into it. Falling into a hay baler would probably have been a death sentence too, because no one could have stopped the baler in time.

Carelessness was always the prime cause of accidents around threshers, balers, silage cutters and sawmills. I once caused a sawyer to suffer significant lacerations to his fingers when I was helping him saw stove wood. He was putting the wood into the saw while I was throwing the cut pieces onto a pile for later hauling to our home for use. As we built up a rhythm, I began to pull the cut pieces away from the saw before they were completely cut. In short order, my pulling drew his hand into the saw and cut his fingers. One time, Mr. Dave, who worked for Dad, was on top of the machine as he usually was, and wanted to get someone's attention. He reached into the grain carrier to get some wheat to throw at that person and alert him, since there was too much noise to yell and be heard. His fingers got caught in the auger and were nearly torn off. Accidents like these taught the whole family that the seriousness of carelessness could not be overemphasized.

Farm animals required special respect relative to the damage they could do. People were killed by horse kicks, so when an experienced person had to walk behind a horse in the stable he always walked against the horse, so if the horse kicked, the person would be pitched and not kicked. Bulls and boars were especially dangerous, as some of them were plain mean. A cow or a sow also would be mean if they thought their young were in danger. Milking could be dangerous if the cow was a kicker, and many were. These were usually hobbled, or some other means of securing them were used to protect the milkers.

Flying, biting insects such as bumblebees and yellow jackets were dangerous in two ways. They may sting you, thus causing serious pain, or they may sting the horses and cause them to run and do damage to the machines or the workers. Alden got stung by a wasp so bad on his lips that we called him a Ubangy for several days, but I do not remember anyone going to a doctor for bee stings, and there were many of them. Bee stings were very painful but were doctored by home remedies.

Floods were a problem along the streams and rivers, but this was of no direct concern to us except it made going to and from grade school difficult because we had to cross Hamburg Run. Droughts were extremely hard on everyone, for during dry spells there was no water to irrigate the crops. We boys hauled water from a nearby pond in dry weather if we could, but usually the ponds would also run dry.

Automobiles, though relatively few in number, were also a danger. Alden got hit by a Model T when he was small and had the imprint of the radiator on his face until he was twelve or fifteen years old. He ran into the car more than the car ran into him as we were running to meet our father when he came home from work.

Diseases such as flu epidemics were of great concern. Grandpa Dellinger died from typhoid fever in a West Virginia bark camp when my mother was five years old. The story of this left a lasting impression.

Another concern was thieves. The prime targets for thieves were our chickens as well as our gas pump located at our driveway and the public road. I remember one night when Mr. Staylor Funkhouser was wiring our house, they thought they heard someone at the chicken house. They went to the chicken house with the shotgun, but found no one. The next morning there was gas missing, so they had gone in the wrong direction. Rigging a shotgun to discharge when someone opened a chicken house or some other door was not unusual.

Making poor or less than expected grades in school was of serious concern to us boys. Mother was a schoolteacher before she married, so we had the advantage of someone to help us and, just as importantly, someone to encourage us to do the best that we could. We were expected to get good grades in all classes, and due to her help, encouragement and pushing, we always did pretty well, although there was always room for improvement. We did many things that we shouldn't have and we got caught at some of these, but there were many that we did not get caught doing. We did not volunteer to talk to our parents about any of the things we did that we shouldn't have done. Our parents did not raise any dumb kids.

There was always the fear of getting sick and not being able to attend school or work during the summer. We never wanted to fail at anything we did, whether it was in school or in our work. We were especially concerned as to what we would do when we finished school and joined the work force on a full-time basis. My Uncle Harry asked me what I wanted to do when I finished high school. I said that I wanted to become an electrician, to which he replied, "If you are sure of what you want to do, you are ahead of me as I still don't know what I want to do." It was years later before I truly understood the full significance of his comment. Incidentally, he was always employed in an apparently interesting, well-paying job.

## Chapter Seventeen

## WHAT TO DO?

Early in my senior year of high school I got serious about the big decision "What to do?" One who already knows what you want to do in life at this age is most fortunate but even then, in many cases, one may be wrong. There are so many facets to a vocation that one may not be aware of, as well as changes to it over time. My problem was that I had no burning desire for any vocation that I was familiar with. In fact, the only vocation I had much knowledge of at all was farming. So you see, I had a minuscule, narrow view of the overall world of opportunity. What to do?

I thought about going to college, but the cost of a college education appeared astronomical. College was occasionally mentioned in high school and possibly by some other people, but without much emphasis. In fact, I can't remember a single high school teacher recommending that I go to college, even though I was in the upper ten percent of the class. Only one person out of our class of forty-nine went directly to college.

The next consideration was to learn a skilled trade. I had, in the back of my mind, a pie-in-the-sky fantasy of going to college after learning a trade and accumulating enough money for college expenses. The question now was "what and how to obtain skilled training?"

I decided not to become a farmer since it would be extremely difficult to own my own farm. I figured it would probably take forever to accumulate enough assets to purchase a farm, not to mention the stock and machinery necessary to make it a viable operation. My only other option for a farming career would have been to work on someone else's farm at daily or monthly rates. Daily pay was one dollar twenty-five cents and monthly pay was about thirty dollars. The monthly pay frequently included other benefits, such as a milk cow, two hogs, a house, feed for the cow and hogs and no real estate taxes. When the possibility of marrying and having children was added in, the chance of real success as a farmer appeared elusive to me.

I had more experience in machinery repair—electrical house circuit repair and electrical appliance repair--than anything else except farming. Repairing broken machinery provided the great satisfaction of putting something back into productive service. We had few electrical appliances, and what we had was very simple and my knowledge thus very elementary. Although I had little knowledge of the fields of machinery repair or electricity, I decided to pursue electrical work.

Sometimes small things have a great impact on shaping our decisions and, in turn, our lives. I may have been influenced when Mr. Staylor Funkhouser wired our home, which gave us so much pleasure, safety and comfort. This opened up the world of radio to us as well as much higher light levels, although most rooms had only one overhead light and a couple of receptacles. Most of our lights were switched, some with three-way switches, but a few of the lights were controlled only by pull chains. Almost everyone looked forward to electricity and indoor plumbing, with the exception of my Grandmother Dellinger. She thought that electricity was too dangerous but believed the kerosene lamps she carried around were safe!

The thought never really entered my mind to take the plumbing route as a vocation. Electricity, it seemed to me, would provide so many possibilities, such as house wiring, power company work, commercial work, telephone systems, entertainment and things I didn't even know about. "What to do?" was decided, now it was "How to do it?"

How to get started on a vocation about which I knew virtually nothing seemed to be a big problem, so I talked to several people who I thought might be able to give me some guidance and encouragement. Those who helped me most were my parents, Dr. Martin, Mr. Swartz and Uncle Claude. Uncle Claude gave me some technical advice even though he was in the mail service and not the technology field. I recognized that if I could get some technical schooling, that training might give me a jump start (no pun intended). I had some savings, but I had no idea how much training might cost. Uncle Claude suggested that I try to get employment with a company that offered a training course. Making contacts was now the problem.

My high school academic work was quite satisfactory as far as it went, but I had little idea of what I needed. I was at a disadvantage because Triplett High School and the other four Shenandoah high schools were class "C" high schools. The three classes of high schools in Virginia were A, B and C, with class A being the best relative to classes, teachers and size. My technical preparation was very limited, even though I took the more difficult courses at my parents' insistence. My school had offered only one year of algebra and no physics or solid geometry. The plane geometry teacher learned along with the students. Chemistry was taught by a beautiful teacher of English. (We also learned some chemistry!)

The only technical high school course offered at my high school was, understandably, agriculture. The general designation was Future Farmers of America (FFA) and this training consisted of courses relative to land care, stock care, all work on the farm including shop work to make or repair farm buildings and machinery. A farmer was relatively self-sufficient and did all his own work relative to the land, crops, machinery and buildings. He also did routine veterinary work for his animals, chickens, turkeys and pets such as cats and dogs.

My father, who was taken out of school after the fifth grade to help support the family, said he wanted me to study more difficult courses because he could teach me all I needed to know about farming. He did, and I enjoyed farm work. My enjoyment was partially due to being able to see the results of one's efforts immediately, in some cases, and after a relatively short time, in other cases. The congeniality and sense of humor of fellow farm workers also made farming interesting and rewarding.

I still had to get a handle on the idea of a lifetime in the electrical world. Uncle Claude helped me in my approach to obtain more knowledge and understanding in this area. He suggested that I contact Coyne Electrical School in Chicago and Bliss Electrical School in Washington, D.C. Both of those schools were well known and the Bliss school was probably the premier school. I contacted Coyne and they recommended that I order their three-volume publication and study it on my own, which would give me access to their write-in question program. The school had been taken over by the armed services to train military personnel. I ordered the book and immediately started to study as they had suggested. This was slow going, since I had no one to ask questions of, but as my father used to say when the hay was poor, "It may not be much but it beats a snowball."

In the spring of 1942 I heard about the Newport News Shipbuilding and Dry Dock Company Apprentice School, which had a four and five year apprenticeship in about thirty trades. A friend of mine, Maxwell Miller from Headquarters community, was serving his apprenticeship in the Steam Engineers at Newport News. He thought the school was great and sent me information on the school including application forms.

The Apprentice School offered college level courses in math, physics, chemistry, drafting, shipbuilding, economics, metallurgy, specific trade technology, and even a course in etiquette. Completion of the apprentice training was supposed to supply the equivalent of two years of college.

I applied to the Apprentice School and gave my three trade preferences as electrical, machinist and sheet metal. Almost all applicants requested both the electrical and machinists trades because these trades had application inside and outside the shipbuilding program. The odds were against a person to get accepted in either the electrical or machinist trade.

The Apprentice School appeared to be the best overall opportunity for me. I made a maximum effort to get accepted. Dr. Martin encouraged me, wrote a letter of recommendation and, I suspect, made other efforts to get me accepted. Mr. Burgess Nelson, our state senator, also wrote a letter of recommendation. Mr. Nelson did not know me personally but my father introduced me to him and after an extensive interview he endorsed me. I was accepted in the Apprentice School in July, 1942, and given a report date of August 12, 1942, to report for work as an apprentice sheet metal worker.

I worked for my Uncle Fred from the time I graduated from high school until I left for Newport News, Virginia, and the Apprentice School. My Uncle had two farms, several saw mills and grazing land. He always treated his employees as if they were important and not just another pair of hands. He always did very well financially and frequently helped deserving people get through some tight spots. I enjoyed working for him and working with his other employees.

The family took me to Mt. Jackson to catch the Greyhound bus to Newport News. There was a transfer to Trailways in Staunton and back to Greyhound in Richmond. My mother especially hated to see me leave, but that was to be expected. I am sure she thought, "He is just seventeen years old, never been away from home except with family, going to a city where he only knows one person and nothing about city life or the kind of work he will be doing." She probably worried whether I could handle it emotionally or physically, what kind of people would I encounter and how would they influence me.

My mother had cause to worry. I transferred to Trailways and put my suitcase on the bus to Richmond, but it still had the check destination of Staunton on it. Somewhere the suitcase was removed from the bus and sent back to Staunton without my knowledge. I did not get the suitcase for six weeks, which left me with no clean clothes. This did not make life easy. I had to get my social security card, which was very frustrating. I was quite homesick and the suitcase and social security problem did not help, but I was not about to throw in the towel and go home. When I finally reported to work at Newport News Shipbuilding I was put in the electrical department, which put everything right. The people I worked for and associated with were extremely helpful and made my new life a great experience.

# EPILOGUE:
## AFTER I LEFT HOME

I entered the apprenticeship program at Newport News Shipbuilding & Dry Dock Company (NNS&DDCO) in August 1942. I was assigned to the electrical department (X31) as a helper prior to actually going into the apprentice School. The electrical apprenticeship was unique, since electrical apprentices were on probation and worked as a helper for up to a year, whereas all other trades accepted the apprentice applicants immediately. A helper received sixty-eight cents per hour and a first year apprentice received sixty-four cents per hour for the first year, and a ten cent raise each year thereafter.

I worked directly for Mr. Earl Smoot, a true gentleman. He later led a group of electricians to scrap up (complete all unfinished electrical items) the first six of the Landing Ship Tanks (LST) ships and I was in this group. This was the first time I ever worked on a ship.

My apprenticeship formally started November, 1942. For the next year and a half I worked in the apprentice training section, yard electrical maintenance in the machine shops and then on the Ticonderoga, an Essex class aircraft carrier. Mr. G. G. Givens (Doc) was in charge of all electrical apprentice training. He was another real gentleman and knew how to develop skilled electrical and electronic technicians.

My "friends and neighbors" selected me to join the military in April, 1944, since most defense deferments were cancelled and more men were needed in the military. Being told that I would be ordered to report for duty within two weeks, I quit my job and went home to visit family and friends. I had taken the Navy "Eddy Test" and passed it. This gave me an entry into the Naval electronics technicians course, which lasted for forty-eight weeks following boot camp at Green Bay Naval Station. A number of the NNS&DDCO apprentices were in this program. Many of them did quite well, which helped them when they returned to complete their apprenticeship and/or went to college.

I entered the Navy June 26, 1944, after an extended wait at home. I went to the Draft Board every week or two to inquire as to why I was not being called up. Most of us young people wanted to get in the service, as patriotism was running high. In addition, if you left defense employment and did not go into service within ninety days, the company had no obligation to re-employ you after the war was over. I worked for my Uncle Fred and also helped in the custom work that both Uncle Fred and my father were engaged in.

I was inducted into the Navy in Roanoke, Virginia, and reported to Green Bay for boot camp. There was one other recruit on the train assigned to the same training course. In our discussions, he stated that he had been teaching physics at the University of Virginia. I thought that with competition like that, I was probably not long for this training school. Boot camp was somewhat a breeze, as I was in good physical condition from my work in the shipyard and on the farm, as well as from good, clean living.

I came home for two weeks leave at the completion of boot camp and had a great time. I was then assigned to Wright Junior College in Chicago for pre-radio training.

At Wright Junior College, we studied math, electrical subjects and support courses such as slide rule use. I had never heard of a slide rule before, much less used one. Most of the trainees were skilled in their use since many of them had several years of electrical engineering. After the first quiz I was assigned extra study for the entire four weeks, but I did not flunk out. I ranked about five hundred in a graduating class of five hundred fifty. The class started with about eight hundred, so we lost a few along the way. These men were assigned to some other naval training program such as electricians. The entire class averaged two to three years of college and most of them in engineering. This compares to my training in a class C high school and one and a half years of the apprenticeship completed. The apprentice training was a tremendous help in getting through this course.

The College of the Ozarks in Clarksville, Arkansas, was my assignment for primary radio school, which lasted three months. Here we studied electronic circuitry, built simple electronic equipment, and took more math and other support courses. Life at the College of the Ozarks, which had been taken over by the Navy, was a delightful experience but the curricula was tough. The liberty and available social life were great, and the townspeople were so good to us. We were on liberty from Saturday noon to Sunday night every week.

The chow hall was contract operated by civilians, therefore we had no chow duty. The food was very good, especially the Arkansas peaches (fruit, that is). The buildings had all been renamed after islands in the Pacific. I lived in the Solomon's. I ranked about sixty out of one hundred twenty in the class, but I studied much harder than the average student due to my limited academic background. At the completion of the primary radio course I was assigned to the Naval Air Technical Training Center (NATTC) at Corpus Christie, Texas. This was for the seven month course in Secondary Radio Tech Training.

The school was located on Ward Island, which was between Corpus Christie and the Naval Base. We lived in barracks on the island and had liberty from noon Saturday until Sunday night, three weekends out of four. The fourth weekend we had duty. My usual weekend liberty activity was to go to Houston one weekend, to San Antonio the next weekend, and back to Houston on the third weekend. The fourth weekend was duty on the base, but we could sometimes go in to Corpus Christi. I took additional trips to nearby places such as Brownsville, Texas, and Matamoras, Mexico. I hitch-hiked everywhere I went. The people were so good about picking us up, and I estimate that I hitch-hiked over ten thousand miles in Texas.

Our NATTC study consisted of over eight hours of classroom and lab work each week day and four hours on Saturday. We had additional study hours at night inside the compound because everything was considered classified. This was good training in security. Our lab work consisted of working on the electronic equipment, the same as that installed on operating naval aircraft. This included radio communications, long range navigation equipment, radar and special equipment such as night fighter gear. I was eighteenth out of a class of one hundred-twenty. If I could have gone to more schools, I may have approached the top of the class. We competed the course late July, 1945.

My next assignment was Norfolk Naval Air Station (NAS) and then to the Pacific for aircraft carrier duty. The dropping of the two atomic bombs about mid-August and the surrender of Japan changed life for most servicemen. I always say that I was in the service but not in the war, as I had no combat experience. I spent the next year at NAS, Norfolk, in carrier air service unit twenty-one (CASU-21) performing maintenance on navy planes such as the F4F, PBY, PBM, F6F, F4U, TBM and TBF. The electronic equipment was communications, LORAN, Sonoboy, Radar (APS-4 and others) and miscellaneous electrical and electronic aircraft gear.

There were about one hundred-twenty technicians to service two air groups. All equipment was given an operations check every thirty hours. The sixty-hour tests required some additional checks compared to the thirty-hour checks. The one hundred twenty-hour check required that all equipment be removed from the plane, bench check each unit, do a complete alignment, reinstall on the plane and check it out with the plane engine running. We ran the planes up ourselves but never moved them under their own power.

Near the time of my discharge we were servicing three air groups with only about thirty technicians. We had to cut our checks short with this difficult workload and few technicians. We never lost a plane as a result of these curtailed checks. The low manpower level was due to the discharge of men from service.

Contrary to what many sailors said about being stationed in Norfolk, I thought the city and liberty were great. I was discharged from the Navy on July 6, 1946.

I returned to my home and helped my brother, Alden, operate Uncle Fred's threshing rig until early September.

The Apprentice School fall classes were to commence in September, so as to prevent any further delay in my apprenticeship, I returned to NNS&DDCO September, 1946. I still had two and a half years to complete the course in the electrical trade.

The remainder of my apprenticeship as an electrician was working electrical systems on aircraft carriers, fruit boats, converting Admiral ships into troop transports and on a PT boat that was being converted to a yacht.

The Apprentice School gave me the opportunity to transfer to the electrical design training course, which extended my apprenticeship to a total of five years. I could complete this extended apprenticeship and still take advantage of the GI Bill for college education. I jointed the active Naval Reserves and was a once-a-month weekend warrior. A single weekend of duty gave me four days' credit and four days' pay. This was a lot of fun and enabled me to keep my skill in servicing naval aircraft electronics.

I completed my apprenticeship January, 1950, and worked as an electrical designer until July, 1950. I enrolled at the University of Virginia Engineering School in Electrical Engineering starting September, 1950. About July, 1950 I received orders to report to naval service in September, 1950, because of the need for skilled electronic technicians for naval aircraft engaged in the Korean war. I quit my job at Newport News, went home to visit, and cancelled my application at the University of Virginia. However, my orders were cancelled when someone realized that if they took all of the skilled technicians out of the reserve squadrons, the squadrons would be very ineffective. I again enrolled at the University of Virginia and commenced classes in September, 1950.

I successfully completed and received my degree in electrical engineering, getting both the power and electronic options. The first two summers I worked for Williams, Coile and Blanchard, an architecture and engineering firm at Newport News. The first summer I was assigned to do the electrical design on an apartment complex in Newport News. Williams, Coile and Blanchard had bought an old school building and were renovating it for their office. I was also assigned the job of doing the electrical design for the renovation. They were able to hire only one apprentice electrician to do the electrical work, and he was inexperienced. I designed the system and helped to install it during the day. I completed my original assignment of the apartment complex at night. The pay associated with the long hours was a tremendous help in my school finances.

The second summer I was assigned the task of surveying the electrical system at the Naval Mine Depot and to design a new system for the future. This was also a very interesting job. The third summer I worked on a government research project at the University of Virginia under Dr. Mase. These summer jobs were learning experiences and were quite helpful in my subsequent job interviews.

I interviewed twelve companies for employment and received eleven offers. I was twenty-nine years old with some very good experience and besides, it was an employees' market. The offers were great, which made it very difficult to decide which one to take. I accepted a job offer from NNS&DDCO in the nuclear engineering field specializing in electrical. This was a relatively new field, appeared interesting, and had a possible bright challenging future. The company sent me to the University of Michigan for 1954 summer school in preparation for nuclear training.

The company then sent me to Oak Ridge School of Reactor Technology at Oak Ridge, Tennessee, in September, 1954. This was the most difficult school I ever attended, as my class standing reflected. Subjects included reactor theory, shielding, nuclear physics, mathematics, fluid systems, steam systems, control systems and laboratory work. These students were extremely intelligent with undergraduate degrees, masters degrees and doctorate in nuclear engineering and nuclear physics. I had much to learn, for I did not even know the nomenclature. Percentage-wise, I probably learned as much as anyone in the class, but it was just that I started with so little.

Our Atomic Power Division was responsible for the shipboard systems associated with a nuclear propulsion plant on a large aircraft carrier, the Enterprise. This was an eight-reactor power plant with two reactors for each propulsion plant. These were as large as any nuclear plant then in construction for land base use. My area of work was to design and develop the electrical generation and distribution system for the power plant and the rest of the ship. We were also responsible for integrating the reactor and instrumentation control system with the rest of the ship's systems.

A full-scale prototype of the number three propulsion plant was built in Idaho to prove the feasibility of a nuclear plant of this size. This was also to be a crew training facility. There were many facets, such as building a generator equal to the power plant output and a power absorbing system to load up the generator. This had to be able to simulate actual ship operation at all conditions from anchor to full speed, both forward and astern. It was a great and rewarding experience.

After the ship was built and delivered, we continued to design paper ships with different reactor designs, different numbers of reactors, etc. The next design selected for a real ship was the Nimitz-class nuclear carrier, which the Navy is still building some thirty years later. These were and are great ships.

Jane Steele and I married December, 1955. She was a music major, graduating from VCU with a masters degree as a music and piano teacher. She was from Purcellville, Virginia. We lived in Newport News until her death fifteen years later. We had no children. I was single for the next five years until Lois Coleman Murphy and I married in 1975. She was widowed in 1973, and had three children by that marriage: Marilyn, Janice and James. I moved to her home and lived there until 2002, when we moved to a retirement community called The Chesapeake.

I retired from the shipyard in 1990 and have been actively involved in avocations since then, just as I was before. One legacy of growing up in the Shenandoah Valley culture I have described herein is that it demanded that a boy develop the ability to be self-sufficient while at the same time it instilled a deeply ingrained habit of helping my neighbors. Even though I have lived in a suburban environment in comparison to the rural environment of my youth, I have always gravitated toward hobbies that were self-supporting. Due to this very practical nature which, incidentally, my entire family shares and perhaps even takes for granted, I have not bought a new car since 1961! In fact, most of my cars have been purchased from salvage yards, rebuilt by me and then used. It is quite rewarding to take a car or other piece of equipment, rebuild it to essentially new condition and then use it for years. Other hobbies I have enjoyed are television, electronics, mechanical, and electrical repairs and, most recently, piano restoration.

We have always had several homes to maintain as well as automobiles and other equipment, so these hobbies have kept me quite busy. I also do work for friends that need some assistance in keeping their cars and homes operating. We seldom have anyone else do any repair work for us. That this philosophy has also been a help for the budget is a bonus!

I have enjoyed solving technical problems with the final results being simple, reliable, low maintenance and inexpensive. An example is when I designed a system to remove water from a friend's basement. Others had proposed using a gasoline-engine-driven generator and an additional electricity-driven sump pump. This method would have required considerable maintenance, would have been relatively expensive and would not have been very reliable.

We installed a dependable inexpensive system using only three basic components. One of these components was static and the other two only had one moving part each. The system functions twenty-four hours a day without needing the attention of the home owner. The expense was less than ten percent of the previously recommended equipment. It was very gratifying to provide a solution to a problem and help someone by doing it.

Despite its somewhat insular environment, I truly believe that growing up in the Shenandoah Valley culture which I have described instilled in me solid values and an ability to take care of myself that I might not have been exposed to elsewhere. Those values and that lifestyle, albeit with the benefit of the more modern conveniences and tools that are now available, live on today in the lives of my relatives in the Shenandoah Valley.

**Figure 18**
Dick, Twyman Elmore, & Alden Bowman

**Figure 19**
Twyman Elmore Bowman & Lois Coleman Murphy
Bowman - 2003

## INDEX

### A

accidents, 14, 128, 180, 201
Anspach, Marilyn and Fred, 5
apples, 65, 69, 87, 111, 112
Apprentice School, 209, 210, 217
architecture, 31
Ashby District, 7, 23, 24
Atomic Power Division, 219
attic, 68, 69, 80, 87, 144
automobile, 104, 138, 176, 182, 184, 198, 200

### B

baling hay, 53
band reunion, 195, 196, 197
bank barn, 46, 52
Barb, George, 56
bark camp, 17, 203
"Bark Edge Bowman", 15
barn threshing, 44, 45
Bauserman, Jim, 131
beans, 92
bedrooms, 62, 67, 74, 80
beef, 81, 97, 98
Belling, 199
belsnickeling, 197
bicycling, 141
binder, 43, 44, 45, 47, 49, 130
black walnuts, 110
blackberry, 57, 111, 114
blacksmith, 24, 35, 130, 182
Bliss Electrical School, 208
Bowman
    Bertie Ellen, 16
    Dick and Barbara, 5, 58, 86
    Dick Delford, 3, 7, 13
    Elizabeth Frances, 14
    Harry Guy, 16
    Ida Rebecca Myers, 14
    James Rufus, 14
    Joseph Earl, 3, 7, 12, 13, 15, 20, 21, 84, 135
    Josephine Dorcas, 14
    Joyce Augusta Dellinger, 7, 18
    Joyce Dellinger, 3, 12, 13
    Lois Coleman Murphy, 5, 223
    Martha Ellen, 14
    Martin Luther, 14
    Mary Virginia, 14
    Philip, 72, 84
    Rebecca Dyer, 14
    Rebecca Mae, 16
    Roy Otis, 15
    Sarah Margaret, 14
    Stella, 18
    Twyman Elmore, 2, 7, 13, 150, 151, 175, 223
    Wilbur Alden, 3, 7, 13
    William Fisher, 14
    William Fred, 15
Bowman's Crossing, 23, 26
brains, 105, 118
bread, 19, 104, 118, 119, 120
bridge, 26, 27, 28, 29, 46, 52, 82, 115, 140, 165, 188
broadcasting, 48
broilers, 107, 108, 118
brooder house, 70, 107, 108
broom corn, 90, 91
Buddy, 170
buggy, 9, 50, 120, 129, 137, 139, 142, 176, 182, 183, 184, 196
bunch beans, 95
bus, 18, 186, 188, 210
butchering, 100

### C

cabbage, 94, 96, 119, 123
"Cabin Hill", 17
cakes, 104, 110, 113, 119, 196, 197
candy, 113, 115, 167, 197
cantaloupes, 94
car, 69, 70, 77, 104, 131, 185, 186, 187, 192, 200, 203, 220
cards, 137
Carpenter, Sarah, 14
carrots, 96, 124, 132
cats, 146, 155, 208
caves, 29
celery, 95, 125

cellar, 59, 64, 65, 73, 78, 90, 92, 94, 95, 96, 106, 111, 112, 125
checking, 38, 152
cherries, 87, 110, 127
chicken, 62, 70, 71, 72, 74, 75, 76, 77, 81, 82, 87, 91, 106, 107, 108, 109, 118, 120, 121, 126, 132, 140, 155, 203
chicken house, 62, 70, 71, 75, 76, 81, 82, 87, 108, 109, 126, 140, 203
chickens and eggs, 106
church, 11, 29, 71, 117, 131, 158, 159, 160, 195, 196
cider, 112, 197
cistern, 59, 60, 61, 63, 68, 70, 74, 78
Civil War, 16
Clanahan, Green, 8, 63, 141
clothing, 190
College of the Ozarks, 214
Conicville, 8, 14, 17, 19, 23, 158, 159, 160, 176
cookies, 110, 113, 114, 121, 197, 199
corn harvesting, 40
corn planting, 37
county fair, 195, 197
cowboys and Indian, 138
cows, 31, 33, 43, 49, 55, 56, 60, 62, 70, 71, 81, 87, 92, 93, 96, 97, 98, 99, 117, 120, 124, 126, 127, 132, 137, 138, 144, 184, 191, 193, 196, 202, 206
cows And milking, 96
Coyne Electrical School, 208
cream, 56, 66, 77, 98, 114, 116, 117, 127, 162, 180, 196, 199
Crop rotation, 34
crows, 152
Cucumbers, 93
cultipackers, 36
cultivation, 24, 38, 39, 88, 91, 123
cultivators, 24, 39

## D

Dellinger
    Charles Peter, 17
    Claude, 18
    Grandmother, 18, 73, 85, 122, 134, 195, 206
    Harold, 19
    Hildred, 19
    Lewis, 167
    Mary Catherine Dodson, 17
    Wilbur ("Wib"), 18
dentist, 113, 179
dining room, 62, 64, 65, 66, 67, 79
disc harrow, 36, 42
discarded farm machinery, 136
discipline, 9, 10, 97, 143, 164, 168
diseases, 177
Dodson
    Charles, 17, 22
    Jackson, 17
    Robert, 17, 22
dog, 55, 66, 153, 168, 192
Dorcas, Ellie and Polly, 18
Downey, Dr., 10, 176, 178, 180
drags, 36
drill, 30, 42, 130

## E

Easter, 145, 162
Eckard's Store, 26
Edinburg, 16, 23, 24, 25, 26, 144, 148, 159, 176, 180
Edinburg Mill, 16, 24
eggs, 31, 65, 71, 98, 107, 108, 109, 118, 119, 120, 125, 145
Electric Power, 29
electricity, 29, 69, 115, 144, 191, 206, 221
exercises, 148

## F

farm management, 32
farm products, 24, 198
farming, 7, 24, 26, 32, 33, 34, 205, 206, 208
fence row, 57, 159
fertilized, 87
festival, 198

UNTIL I LEFT HOME 227

field threshing, 45
fire, 31, 50, 65, 66, 67, 80, 92,
   101, 103, 104, 107, 115, 120,
   139, 141, 143, 144, 167, 179,
   195, 196, 199, 200, 201
fire carnivals, 143, 195
fish, 99, 118, 140, 146
Foltz
   Douglas, 5
   Margaret, 15
   Pearl, 14
Foltz's Store, 26
food, 87
Frederick County, 23
frog gigging, 154
frog hunting, 140, 155
frogs, 146, 152, 154
Frontier Cultural Center, 31
fruits, 87
furniture, 10, 66, 67, 79

### G

garden, 17, 18, 32, 33, 60, 71,
   75, 87, 88, 89, 94, 95, 96,
   122, 125, 126, 139, 144, 154,
   181
general stores, 26
Givens, G. G., 212
Gochenour Farm, 131
grain harvesting, 43
grain planting, 42
grain threshing, 44
Grim, Mollie, 14
guns, 137, 153

### H

Hamburg Grade School, 162
hand corn chopper, 40
hand plow, 123
Hardy County, 23
Harrisonburg, 8, 23, 133, 176,
   177
Hawkinstown, 23, 159
hay baler, 8, 53, 201
hay making, 46, 48
hay rick, 49, 51
hay tedders, 49
Headquarters, 23, 158, 209

heating, 30
Heishman, Lucinda, 14
Hite, Issac, 78
hog pen, 62, 70, 77, 99, 101, 127
hogs, 24, 26, 32, 33, 40, 41, 43,
   60, 62, 66, 70, 71, 77, 98, 99,
   100, 101, 102, 103, 118, 127,
   144, 188, 198, 206
Hollar, Sam, 139
homemade soap, 191
horses, 31, 34, 35, 37, 39, 41,
   42, 43, 46, 49, 50, 51, 52, 54,
   56, 78, 81, 90, 91, 117, 130,
   138, 141, 144, 147, 165, 182,
   187, 198, 202
horseshoes, 138, 147
hospitals, 176
hunting, 152

### I

ice cream, 98, 116, 117
ice houses, 117
ice-skating, 141
illness, 18, 72, 155, 176
indoor plumbing, 64, 206
Insect control, 125
insects, 53, 202

### J

jelly, 92, 112, 114
Jerome, 8
Johnson District, 23

### K

kitchen, 10, 30, 62, 63, 64, 65,
   66, 73, 74, 75, 77, 78, 79, 80,
   87, 115, 162, 192
"Knot Hole Brown", 15

### L

lawn parties, 143, 195, 196
leeks, 96
lettuce, 96, 119
lima beans, 93
Lindamood, Eugene, 64

living room, 62, 66, 67, 74, 77, 78, 79, 80, 127
Long, Joe, 170
Lorenz, Janice Murphy, 5
Lower Hamburg, 7, 26
lumberyard, 15
Lutz, Ellie, 18

## M

machinery, 7, 8, 24, 25, 33, 82, 130, 136, 137, 147, 185, 190, 198, 201, 205, 206, 208
Madison College Teachers Normal, 8
manure spreader, 56
marbles, 148
Martin, Dr., 179, 207, 209
mechanical hay loader, 52
medical care, 176
milking, 34, 55, 56, 87, 97, 98
Mill Creek, 25, 28
miscellaneous farming tasks, 54
movie, 148
mow, 49, 50, 52, 53, 82, 129, 131
Mt. Jackson, 15, 16, 18, 23, 25, 26, 27, 29, 31, 98, 117, 120, 133, 139, 171, 174, 179, 188, 196, 198, 210
Mt. Pleasant, 23
Murphy
    Jim and Christion, 5
    Lois Coleman, 5, 220, 223
muskrats, 152, 169
mutton, 98
Myers
    John, 14, 56
    Tom, 14

## N

National Business College, 16
Naval Air Technical Training Center, 215
Naval Mine Depot, 218
Navy, 213, 214, 216, 220
Nelson, Burgess, 209
New Market, 23
New York City, 146, 185, 188

Newport News, 72, 209, 210, 211, 212, 217, 218, 220
Newport News Shipbuilding and Dry Dock Company Apprentice School, 209
Norfolk, 215, 216
Norfolk Naval Air Station, 215
North Fork, 25, 113
nuts, fruits, berries and melons, 110

## O

Oak Ridge School of Reactor Technology, 219
Old Maid, 137
one-horse buggy rake, 50
onions, 96, 119
opossums, 72, 152, 153
organ, 74, 159, 195
Otterbein Chapel, 117, 159, 160, 161
our garden, 87

## P

Page County, 23
Painters Store, 26
parlor, 62, 64, 73, 80, 195, 200
parsley, 96
parsnips, 96, 119, 124
peaches, 87, 111, 121, 214
peppers, 96
phone, 80
picnics, 143
pies, 92, 98, 110, 111, 113, 114, 196
Pig, 137
pigeons, 140, 152, 157
pigs, 87, 99, 127
play, 27, 94, 116, 136, 137, 138, 140, 141, 143, 145, 147, 148, 169, 170, 192, 195
plow, 34, 35, 38, 39, 88, 89, 90, 123, 124, 125, 129, 139, 187
plowing, 34
poison ivy, 57
poison oak, 57
pon haus, 104

## UNTIL I LEFT HOME  229

popcorn, 115
popcorn balls, 113, 116
porch, 16, 59, 64, 65, 73, 74, 78, 80, 95, 124, 127, 163
pork, 65, 118, 120, 121
possum, 152
potato bugs, 89, 125
potatoes, 65, 67, 79, 88, 89, 90, 93, 94, 118, 119, 122, 123, 125
poundings, 200
privy, 64, 70
Protestant, 30, 158
puddin meat, 104
Pugh's Run, 132
pullets, 108
pumpkins, 65, 67, 71, 92

### R

rabbit fever (tularemia), 76
rabbits, 152, 155, 156, 169
radio, 66, 79, 144, 185, 206, 213, 214, 215
radishes, 96
railroad, 17, 131, 171, 186, 188
restaurant, 120
ricker, 48
Rinkerton, 23
road wagon, 182, 183
Roanoke College, 16
Rochelle Grade School, 9
Rockingham County, 23
Rook, 137
roosters, 108
Rosenberger, Edgar, 26
Route 614, 23, 26, 59, 76

### S

Salem Church, 131, 147, 159
salsify, 96, 119
Salyer, Ray, 5
Saturday night bath, 63
sawmills, 7, 8, 15, 81, 201
scenic points, 31
school, 7, 8, 9, 10, 14, 29, 104, 112, 118, 120, 121, 122, 129, 136, 143, 145, 148, 158, 159, 162, 163, 164, 165, 166, 167, 168, 169, 170, 171, 172, 179, 184, 186, 190, 192, 193, 194, 195, 196, 200, 203, 204, 205, 207, 208, 209, 210, 213, 214, 215, 218, 219
sewing machine, 66, 190
Shenandoah River, 23, 25, 28, 31, 113, 189
shocked, 41, 42, 113
Shutters, Celia, 18
sickle-bar mower, 48
silage, 37, 201
silo, 10, 32, 40, 46, 70, 81, 82, 107, 129
skunks, 152, 153, 169
sledding, 142
smoke house, 62, 68, 69, 81, 100, 103, 106, 112
Smoot, Earl, 212
snow, 9, 28, 41, 59, 68, 71, 142, 143, 155, 187, 188, 194
snow brakes, 71
socializing, 143, 195, 196, 198, 200
South Fork, 25
sports, 143
spring wagon, 182
squirrels, 152, 155, 156
stables, 56, 82
steam engine, 8, 45, 53
Stoney Creek, 25, 28
Stout, Kathryn, 16
stove, 62, 65, 66, 67, 68, 73, 74, 75, 77, 79, 107, 108, 115, 119, 162, 170, 178, 192, 201
Strasburg, 23, 31
straw fork, 56
straw hats, 193
strawberries, 96
Stud Horse Cart, 139, 184
sugar, 87
Sundays, 30, 34, 121
surgery, 177
surrey, 165, 184
sweet corn, 91
sweet potato, 93
sweets and snacks, 113
swimming, 140

## T

taffy, 114, 115, 116
telephone, 79, 80, 207
thieves, 68, 109, 203
thinning, 38, 39, 128, 131
toboggans, 193
tomatoes, 94, 124
toys, 97, 144
traction engine, 8
trade, 205, 209, 217
train, 139, 188, 208, 213
trapping, 152
trash pile, 83
travel and transportation, 182
Triplett High School, 14, 162, 171, 174, 186, 207
trucks, 189
turtles, 152
two-hole privy, 62, 70, 75
two-horse side-delivery rake, 50
typhoid fever, 17, 203

## U

United Brethren Church, 159, 160
University of Virginia, 16, 213, 217, 218
Upper Hamburg, 7, 15

## V

vegetables, 87

vocation, 205, 207
"Voss" wringer washer, 69

## W

wagons, 182
wash house, 54, 62, 68, 69, 70, 71, 78, 102
Washington, D.C., 18, 19, 108, 145, 188, 208
water, 30, 40, 59, 61, 108
Waterman, George, 64, 78
watermelons, 113
Weatherholz, Lena, 63
Williams, Coile and Blanchard, 218
Winchester, 23, 176, 198
windrows, 50
Woodstock, 14, 23, 131, 179
work, 7, 8, 9, 10, 15, 18, 30, 32, 33, 34, 39, 52, 53, 54, 57, 69, 79, 89, 91, 100, 120, 122, 124, 125, 127, 128, 129, 132, 133, 136, 138, 141, 148, 159, 162, 164, 171, 179, 185, 192, 195, 203, 204, 206, 207, 208, 210, 211, 213, 215, 218, 219, 221
Wright Junior College, 213, 214
Wunder, Dr., 179

## Z

Zirkle, Clarence, 16